LENINGRAD 1941

LENINGRAD 1941

THE BLOCKADE

DMITRI V. PAVLOV

TRANSLATED BY JOHN CLINTON ADAMS

FOREWORD BY HARRISON E. SALISBURY

THE UNIVERSITY OF CHICAGO PRESS

CHICAGO & LONDON

Library of Congress Catalog Card Number: 65-24979

THE UNIVERSITY OF CHICAGO PRESS, CHICAGO & LONDON
The University of Toronto Press, Toronto 5, Canada

THE STRONG IN HEART
ARE INVINCIBLE

AUTHOR'S NOTE

FROM THE BEGINNING of the siege of Leningrad until the end of January, 1942, I was stationed in Leningrad, dealing with problems of food supply for the population of the city and the armed forces. I have preserved some notes and documents of that time which enable me to tell somewhat more fully than what has been published until now how the people of Leningrad were fed during those grim days, to discuss problems of food supply, and to describe in greater detail than heretofore the organization of the supply service for the population of the city and the troops of the Leningrad Front during the worst days of the blockade.

Military operations, road building, and the struggle to maintain communications are mentioned in my account only as the background against which the life and activities of the besieged are portrayed during the most difficult months of the blockade. The conclusions and critical observations I make in the course of my narrative of events are based on my impressions as I lived through the difficult days of siege and on my judgment of events from the vantage point of the present.

The second edition of the book contains additional information and data relating to the latter half of 1941 which make possible a somewhat fuller description of the actual conditions under which the city's defenders contended with the Fascist enemy and with hunger during the critical days of the siege.

What is said by no means exhausts the subject of the courage and efficiency of the city's defenders and of the population, who endured such a long siege under desperate conditions.

CONTENTS

ILLUSTRATIONS

FIGURES

(following pages 88 and 120)

MAPS

xi

FOREWORD

HARRISON E. SALISBURY

LATE IN THE SPRING of 1958 there appeared in the bookshops of some Soviet cities, including Moscow and Leningrad, a slim 164-page volume, bound in gray-blue linen, called *Leningrad v Blokade*. The author of the work was Dmitri Vasilevich Pavlov, who was identified in a brief note as the representative of the State Committee for Defense in charge of food supplies for the Leningrad Front and the Leningrad population from the beginning of the siege of Leningrad to the end of January, 1942.

The book bore the imprimatur of the Military Publishing House of the Soviet Defense Ministry, but it was not published by the principal press of the House, located in Moscow. It was issued by the smaller Second Typography named for Voroshilov which is in Leningrad.

Although the *tirage* or number of copies printed is published in almost every Soviet book, along with the Censorship Office approval number, this figure was omitted from the publication data appearing in the Pavlov volume, a practically certain sign that the original print order was very small, quite possibly not more than two or three thousand.

Even in so tiny an edition, however, the appearance of Pavlov's book caused great excitement. Thirteen years had passed since the end of World War II, and still many of the basic facts about the siege of Leningrad, surely one of the epics of man's experiences in war, were unknown even within the Soviet Union. These facts Pavlov's book at long last made public.

The city of Leningrad encompassed about 2,544,000 persons, including some 400,000 children, when its last land connections with Russian-held territory were severed by the Germans on September 8, 1941. In addition, an estimated 343,000 persons lived in suburban and other nearby areas within the siege lines. And not until 872 days had passed, just short of two and one-half years, was the siege fully lifted and the city's normal communications and supply routes re-established.

During the siege an estimated 632,000 persons died of hunger, cold, and related dystrophic causes. This figure is distinct from deaths due to purely military causes such as German bombing and shelling. Nor do these figures include the battlefield casualties. Unofficial estimates of the total Leningrad dead have run in the area of 1,000,000. Mikhail Dudin, a prominent Leningrad writer, estimated in March of 1965 that the total was 1,100,000.[1]

These statistics alone give to the siege of Leningrad a unique position in the history of modern warfare. The famous siege of Paris, for example, lasted only four months from September 19, 1870, to mid-January, 1871. The siege of Vicksburg in the American Civil War endured from May 18 to July 4, 1863. In neither instance was a population comparable to Leningrad's involved. Nor did either include such complications as the Russian winter (temperatures of 20 and 30 below zero in a virtually heatless, lightless city), the constant accompaniment of Nazi air attack and artillery bombardment, and the paralysis of the transport and communications facilities of a city of 65,000 acres, served on the eve of the war by 327 miles of tram lines and 206 miles of bus routes.

The story of Leningrad's heroic ordeal went so long untold for several reasons. Except for the ephemeral journalism of wartime and a few slight pamphlets, very little was published about the Soviet war effort until after the death of J. V. Stalin on March 5, 1953. Only one study of serious value appeared—Nikolai Voznesensky's *War Economy of the Soviet Union,* published in 1948—and it was quickly suppressed. The author, a member of

[1] *Literaturnaya Gazeta,* March 27, 1965.

the Politburo, was arrested and shot. This served to discourage even the most casual kind of historical research.

Another factor severely blighted any effort to tell the Leningrad story. The Leningrad political organization, headed by A. A. Zhdanov, was deeply involved in the labyrinthine power intrigues of the Kremlin. With the death of Zhdanov, August 31, 1948, a quiet, unpublicized, but pervasive effort was set in motion to minimize and even suppress public notice of Leningrad's heroic achievements.

For example, as Pavlov writes with great bitterness, the Leningrad Museum of Defense, which had been opened after the war and which was dedicated to the city's epic siege, was liquidated in 1949 and it appears that not all of the materials then dispersed have yet been re-collected. A Museum of History was opened in 1957 and some of the materials are to be found there. But, as Pavlov emphasizes, the deficit has not yet been made good.

Other examples of suppression of Leningrad's story have come to light since Pavlov wrote.

Perhaps the most notable of these was the fate of a work prepared by the Leningrad House of Scientists under the general direction of Academician I. A. Orbeli, dealing with the achievements of Leningrad science during the blockade years. The work appears to have been completed shortly after the end of the war, but "for a series of reasons" it was not published and now exists only in the form of two collections of proof sheets, one preserved in the Leningrad Public Library and the other in the Archives of the USSR Academy of Science.[2]

As a consequence of such suppression, in the bibliographies relating to Leningrad's war effort, the entries prior to 1953 are extremely scanty except for a few writers' diaries and scattered brochures dealing with fragments of the panoramic events. And, curiously, the lacuna was not immediately filled after Stalin's death. There was, quite obviously, a political hangover resulting from the fierce quarrel in which Leningrad and its political apparatus had been involved.

[2] A. V. Koltzov, *Uchenye Leningrada v Godi Blokadi 1941–43* (Leningrad, 1961). Koltzov notes that the proof carries the date April 15, 1946, and the notation "second proof."

Not until Premier Khrushchev's "secret" speech of February 25–26, 1956, was it confirmed that most of the Leningrad party leadership had been destroyed in the secret purge which followed Zhdanov's death. Among those who lost their lives in this purge were most of the city leaders whose active roles in Leningrad's defense are described by Pavlov—A. A. Kuznetzov, Ya. F. Kapustin, P. S. Popkov, and many, many others. Voznesensky, too, was a member of the so-called "Leningrad Group" and one of the victims of what is known now as the "Leningrad Affair."

It is not surprising, then, to find that A. V. Karasev, author of probably the most scholarly work yet to appear on the Leningrad siege, finds as late as 1958 that there is an absence of "fundamental research about the work and achievements of the workers of Leningrad during the blockade" and that "for a number of reasons" studies which have appeared have lacked basic facts and statistics.[3]

Pavlov's book, appearing in that same year of 1958, was the first to supply those "basic facts and statistics." Little is known about the circumstances of its writing and publication. Leningrad celebrated the 250th anniversary of its founding in 1957 (four years late). A considerable number of popular accounts of the siege of Leningrad were published for that occasion, most notably a collection of wartime reminiscences and diaries, many of which had been published during the war, under the title *900 Days*. This work, however, and most of the others issued in connection with the 1957 celebration were submitted for publication and cleared by the Censorship Office late in 1956 and early in 1957. But Pavlov's book was not sent to the printer until early January, 1958, a full year later.

The works prepared for the 1957 celebration, generally, broke little new ground. For the most part they merely republished the skimpy materials of wartime days or glossed over the hardships and difficulties of the extraordinary siege in propagandistic fashion. Not so with Pavlov. In almost every page of his book he presents facts, figures, and statistics of the most intimate kind, relating to the incredible difficulties of attempting to maintain the life

[3] A. V. Karasev, *Leningradtzi v Godi Blokadi* (Moscow, 1959).

of a metropolitan city when it has been deprived of normal means of obtaining foodstuffs, fuel, and power for light and energy.

Here for the first time are published the actual quantities of foodstuffs at the disposal of the authorities at the beginning of the crisis and an almost weekly account of their diminishing. Pavlov presents the details of each difficult decision and situation which the city faced: the successive cuts in rations (which by November 20, 1941, had dropped to 250 grams of bread daily for a worker, 125 grams for office employees, dependents, and children); the rapidly changing formula employed in making bread (by the end of November it comprised the following: edible cellulose 10 per cent, cottonseed cake 10 per cent, chaff 2 per cent, meal dust from old sacks 2 per cent, corn flour 3 per cent, rye flour 73 per cent), and the rapidly rising toll of cold and starvation—11,085 deaths in November; 52,881 in December; 199,187 in January and February of 1942.

For the first time Pavlov presented actual tonnage figures for the "Road of Life"—the ice road constructed over frozen Lake Ladoga—which gave Leningrad a tenuous link with the outer world from the moment it was put into service on November 23, 1941. The figures, incidentally, revealed that not until well after January 1, 1942, did shipments via Ladoga reach a daily level which insured Leningrad's survival, taking into account the sharply reduced levels of consumption that resulted from the enormous death toll.

From other published works about the siege of Leningrad it would appear that most of the statistics presented by Pavlov are available in the Leningrad archives in one form or another. Most but not all: Pavlov points out in his introduction that his book is based in part upon "some notes and documents" which he preserved from the blockade days and which reveal the "factual resources of food products in the most difficult days of the blockade." It seems clear that Pavlov's sources and conclusions are not to be matched from any other quarter. Every Soviet work bearing on this subject since 1958 has drawn liberally upon his data.

Three years after the small original edition was published, a second and revised version—of which this book is a translation—

was approved for publication in an edition of 50,000 copies, which number was probably in fair accord with readers' demands. Both editions immediately became standard reference works not only for Soviet historians but for foreign scholars dealing with the subject of Leningrad.

It is notable that study of the second edition shows no changes whatsoever in data relative to food supply, although a few corrections are made in minor matters such as the number of air raids, bombs dropped, and fires started on particular nights, apparently reflecting more detailed examination of area reports submitted by fire brigades and ARP units.

The principal difference between the first and second editions lies in the addition of supplementary materials. These are of two kinds. The first edition presents an unpretentious, almost unadorned report, based very largely on the author's own observations. There is little generalization about the war and no particular attempt to sketch in the siege of Leningrad against the greater background of the whole Soviet war effort. In the second edition a number of passages are inserted to supply a little of this background and perspective.

Another kind of material has been added—encomiums for several officials who played a role of one sort or another in the Leningrad blockade. Among the officials who receive such treatment are Anastas I. Mikoyan, now chairman of the Presidium of the Supreme Soviet of the USSR, then a member of the State Committee for Defense; T. F. Shtykov, then a secretary of the Leningrad area party committee in charge of freight transportation, including food; Alexei N. Kosygin, now premier, then a member of the Politburo charged with evacuation of refugees; I. A. Andreenko, a deputy in the Leningrad City Trade Administration. There are also occasional insertions of descriptions of heroic actions by various individuals engaged in civil defense and supplying the city.

Pavlov performs another service in his second edition. He has read many of the works written about the blockade of Leningrad, including some of the fictional accounts of the city's ordeal. He corrects a number of authors for inaccurate detail, even finding an error in the extremely careful work of Karasev.

All this having been said, Pavlov's book still might not be as readable and exciting as it is were it not for another quality. Pavlov writes not as a cool and distant observer. He writes as an angry man. The blockade days were a time of epic heroism. But they were also a time of bungling and blundering, especially in the first weeks of war, which cost thousands of lives. The errors and stupidities with which Pavlov is concerned are not military ones, not those occurring at the front but at the rear. They include, for example, the failure to press forward vigorously with a program for enforced evacuation of children, dependents, and all other civilians not needed for the conduct of the war. This alone cost uncounted lives in the autumn and winter of 1941–42.

Children had been evacuated in June and July, but directly into the path of the Nazi assault. They were sent to Luga, Tolmachevo, and Gatchina. Why? Because there were children's rest homes at those places and, also, the children would be not too far from their parents. A large number of children were lost to the enemy; others had painfully to be returned to Leningrad for re-evacuation, and before many of these could be sent to safety the iron circle closed, and they were trapped within the blockade lines.

But it was not merely a matter of children. Pavlov estimates that not more than 400,000 persons were evacuated from Leningrad during July and August, i.e., before the closing of the escape routes. At least in part this was the fault of party officials themselves who took pride in saying: "Our population is ready to work in the front lines and it will not leave Leningrad." Consequently, the plans for evacuation were not fulfilled; workers were permitted, if not encouraged, to stay at their posts; civilians eager to leave were branded "deserters"; there was no real perception of the danger to all created by permitting the large population to remain in the city.

The same unrealistic attitude obtained in regard to essential food and fuel supplies. Although Pavlov does not state it flatly, he strongly implies that this lack of clear thinking persisted until he was sent by the State Defense Committee to Leningrad on September 8 to assume charge of all food supplies for the city and the troops defending it.

For example, until September 2, Leningrad was on the same rationing system as the rest of the country—workers received 800 grams of bread daily, employees 600, dependents and children 400. With fairly ample rations of meat, cereals, fats, and sugars these amounts were more than adequate. Worse yet, at the time Pavlov took charge Leningrad restaurants and cafés, where food could be obtained without ration cards, continued to function and a good many products were still being sold freely in stores, and farmers' markets. Only on September 2 was the Leningrad ration cut for the first time—to 600 grams of bread daily for workers, 400 for employees, 300 for dependents and children. At this rate the city was consuming 2,000 tons of flour daily and the amount on hand in the civilian system on September 6 was sufficient for only 14.1 days (However, a tally made on September 12, apparently at Pavlov's order, of all the flour, grain, and grain products found thirty-five days' supply, taking civil and military reserves together.)

In the face of this mounting danger, normal peacetime Soviet bureaucracy continued in full flower. For example, in mid-September the Administration of the Sugar Industry in Moscow instructed its Leningrad branch to ship a number of carloads of sugar to Vologda although the last rail link between Leningrad and the rest of Russia had been cut September 8. Food and other essential supplies were controlled by hundreds of different bureaus and bodies, many of which continued to follow "business as usual" practices. Supplemental rations and supplies were issued freely—so freely that in September and October some 2,500 tons of sugar and 600 tons of fats were squandered in this manner. These foods would have saved many lives had they been available in December and January.

One of the most disastrous events of the siege of Leningrad occurred on September 7 and 8, when in the course of mass air attacks on the city, the Germans started large fires in the so-called Badaev warehouses. These were a series of large wooden storehouses, built before 1914 by the St. Petersburg merchant firm of Rasteryaev. The buildings stood not more than thirty feet apart, and fires spread swiftly from one structure to another. Losses were not great in the fires started on September 7, because most of the burned warehouses were vacant. But on September 8 the Germans were more successful; they set fire to buildings in which large quantities of flour and sugar were stored.

In most accounts of the siege of Leningrad, the Badaev fire is blamed for much of the hunger and starvation that followed. Leningrad authorities have been much criticized for permitting such large accumulations of food to remain in one location, easily subject to enemy bombing and almost certain to result in serious loss in event of fire.

Pavlov takes very sharp issue with this view. He estimates the losses at Badaev at no more than 3,000 tons of flour and about 2,500 tons of sugar. He points out that about 700 tons of the sugar were later recovered and reworked for use during the worst days of hunger. The losses were serious but by no means decisive. The squandering of food reserves in the early weeks of the war and, most of all, the failure to evacuate the civilian population in time were the really critical factors, as Pavlov clearly demonstrates.

Pavlov does not gloss over many of the dark episodes in Leningrad. He does not pretend that all Leningraders were heroes. He describes incidents of black marketing, and of theft and forgery of ration cards; he comments on the terrible hardships imposed upon the civilians by the strict rules enforced in November and December when, because of the enormous frauds that previously had prevailed, it was made almost impossible to obtain a new ration card if one was lost or destroyed. Loss of the card then became virtually a sentence to death from starvation, because scanty as the rations were, they were the only source of food.

Pavlov also presents a realistic picture of the disorganization which attended the establishment of the Ladoga Ice Road and the enormous difficulties which had to be overcome before it was made to work with the required efficiency. Like other writers on the subject he makes it plain that if the Soviet Army had not recaptured the vital Tikhvin rail junction on December 9, 1941 (after it had been in German hands a month), Leningrad would have starved to death as the Nazis intended that it should. A round-about road through wilderness country was roughed out in late November. Theoretically, trucks following this 320-kilometer route could have brought in enough supplies to keep the city going. Actually, as experience with the far shorter Ladoga route was to demonstrate, the expedient could not have succeeded. Fortunately, with the recapture of Tikhvin the roundabout route never had to be tested.

Stalin's apparent antipathy toward Leningrad showed itself in the savage intrigues and plots which he directed against various leadership groups in the city, beginning with the assassination of Sergei Kirov, the Leningrad party chief, on December 1, 1934; in the subsequent purge of the Leningrad party, and the city's industrial and military leadership; and in the variety of measures, administrative and otherwise, by which Stalin sought to reduce the prestige and importance of the former Russian capital. Because of all this, it has long been suspected—even publicly alleged by some anti-Soviet critics—that Stalin deliberately permitted Leningrad to fall under prolonged siege and allowed the population to be wiped out in incredible numbers as an act of political vengeance or in furtherance of some long-range political objectives.

Pavlov casts little light on this hypothesis. But he does cite at least one instance of what he regarded as dangerous and unwarranted interference in Leningrad's efforts to organize its defense effort. On August 20 the Military Council of the Northwestern Front (the Leningrad Front) approved a plan to set up a Military Council for Leningrad Defense which would concern itself largely with civil defense, organization of fortifications, formation and training of the militia, and the handling of supplies. The idea was to free Marshal Klimenti Voroshilov and party chief A. A. Zhdanov, who were conducting the military battle against the Germans, from the added responsibility for the internal organization of the city. Stalin vetoed this plan. He insisted that Voroshilov and Zhdanov participate in both councils. As a result the Leningrad Defense Council played no effective role, and the organization of the city's defenses was severely handicapped.

It is typical of the value of Pavlov's work that this instance of Stalin's interference with Leningrad defense arrangements had never been publicly mentioned until reported in his book. And his reference remains that which is cited in all standard Soviet works on Leningrad.

The role of Zhdanov is another prickly subject on which Pavlov is not overly illuminating. He mentions the Leningrad party chief many times. He quotes rather fully from a number of Zhdanov's public speeches and, occasionally, from his own notes of remarks made by Zhdanov on private occasions. But his picture of Zhdanov remains entirely official, unlike his portraits of some others involved in the defense of Leningrad. Within the city both during and after the siege, Zhdanov was the central figure—the hero who had led the city through its ordeal or the villain of its tragedy, depending on the viewpoint of the individual. Although Pavlov provides some slight hints of a conflict in views between Zhdanov and Stalin, he casts no real light on this subject. Visitors to Leningrad during World War II often noted that whereas elsewhere in Russia Stalin was the central figure in the iconography, in Leningrad his place was taken by Zhdanov. It was Zhdanov's portraits, quotations, and slogans which were to be seen throughout the city, not Stalin's. A close reading of Pavlov merely confirms the belief that much of the wartime politics in and concerning Leningrad has yet to be disclosed.

To the extent that Pavlov was involved in those politics, he managed to remain on the surviving side. Born in 1905 and graduated in 1936 from the All-Union Academy of Foreign Trade, he has made his career in government service entirely in the field of food supply and production. His responsibilities in Leningrad began with the inception of the siege in September and continued to the end of January, 1942, by which time the worst of the city's difficulties were in a fair way toward solution. He served throughout the war in the Main Administration of Food Supplies of the Commissariat of Defense. For a period of time he was Minister of Food Industries of the Soviet Union. He has also served as Minister of Trade. In recent years he has held the post of Trade Minister of the Russian Republic. His governmental and political career has been carried forward largely in the train of Anastas I. Mikoyan and Alexei N. Kosygin.

To the world outside the Soviet Union, and to history, Pavlov's major service has been the writing of this book on the siege of Leningrad, which here is translated into English for the first time.

1

THE GERMAN ADVANCE
IN THE NORTHWEST
June–September, 1941

BEHIND THE SCREEN of war with the Western powers, Nazi Germany was secretly preparing an underhanded attack on the USSR. The stunning success of German forces in the west had convinced Hitler that he could win the same sort of victory in a war against the Soviet Union. In December, 1940, at a secret meeting with his army commanders, he had declared: "We can expect that at the very first blow by German forces the Russian army will suffer an even greater defeat than the French army in 1940."[1] During the spring of 1941 the Germans deployed 153 first-class divisions on their eastern frontier; in June they transferred a whole air command from west to east. On the morning of June 22, early, at the orders of the German government, Fascist forces from the Baltic to the Black Sea fell upon the borders of the USSR and drove deep into its territory along previously designated lines of penetration.

For various reasons, military operations began under exceptionally unfavorable conditions for the USSR. The sudden, concentrated blow of the fully mobilized and well-equipped Fascist army placed the troops of our frontier commands in an extremely difficult position. The strategic initiative was the enemy's from

[1] *Lessons of the Second World War* (Moscow: Foreign Literature Publishing House, 1957), p. 73. This work is a translation from the German. [Pavlov's language in the next sentence is ambiguous. Operation Barbarossa was in fact supported by three air commands.—Ed.]

the first days of the war. The future of our motherland hung in the balance. The war immediately assumed an unusually fierce character.

The German forces were divided into three Army Groups: North, Center, and South. We shall follow briefly the military operations of Army Group North, whose area of concentration was East Prussia. It was composed of the German Sixteenth and Eighteenth armies and the Fourth Panzer Group, totaling twenty-nine divisions and more than 500,000 men. The troops were armed extremely well and were equipped with the latest means of communication. Hitler had appointed Field Marshal Von Leeb to command Army Group North.

Leeb, born in 1876, had commanded Germany's Seventh Military District with the rank of lieutenant general before Hitler's coming to power. Documents indicate that Hitler was cool toward him because of his religious convictions, his sharp tongue, and his unfriendly remarks about the National Socialists. In view of his professional qualifications, however, and the support he had in the officers' corps as one of "the old guard of the imperial officer class," Hitler had made him commander of the Second Army Group. Leeb took part in the occupation of the Sudetenland in 1938. In 1940 he was promoted to the command of Army Group "C." Under his leadership, German troops broke through the Maginot Line. For his share in the victory over France, Leeb was ceremoniously promoted to the rank of Field Marshal in July, 1940, and awarded the Knight's Cross. Holding Leeb to be an able general, Hitler intrusted him with the responsibility for carrying out the plan of attack on the Soviet Union in the northwestern sector.

Leeb's mission was to destroy Soviet units stationed in the Baltic area and to launch a rapid offensive by way of Dvinsk-Pskov-Luga, capturing all naval bases on the Baltic and taking Leningrad by July 21. Anxious to justify Hitler's confidence in him, Leeb moved rapidly to carry out his part of Operation Barbarossa.

Morale was very high among the officers and men of the German army. They regarded themselves and the army as Goliaths who could throw aside all obstacles in their path. Actively *re-*

2

vanchist, they were encouraged and inflamed by press and radio and by the speeches of Fascist politicians, who urged their army on into the vast spaces of the East toward new victories, plunder, and rapine.

On June 22 the enemy fell upon the covering forces of the Soviet Eighth and Eleventh armies. The blow was unexpected and so powerful that our troops soon lost contact with their army headquarters. The forces of the advancing enemy were too sizable for the scattered Soviet units, who could not stop the Fascists despite bravery and coolness under fire. By the end of the first day of hostilities, elements of the enemy Fourth Panzer Group had broken through Soviet defenses and were pushing forward.

On the first day of the war the Baltic Military District was reorganized as the "Northwestern Front." It comprised twelve rifle divisions, two motorized, and four armored divisions. These forces were inferior to Leeb's advancing army group numerically and in tanks, automatic weapons, and, in particular, aircraft. The enemy's principal advantage, however, was his ability to attack our units piecemeal, exploiting the fact that the main Soviet forces were far from the frontier and dispersed. Construction of fortified zones at Libau, Schauljai, and elsewhere[2] had not been completed when Hitler attacked. The solidly concentrated forces of the enemy were initially engaged only by covering detachments of the Northwestern Front, then by motorized units, and finally by reserves which were reaching the front five to seven days after the start of the war from distant peacetime locations. This deployment of our troops gave the German Fascist forces clear superiority in strength and contributed to their victories, although they suffered heavy losses in the process.

Soviet operations were further complicated by the clogging of all roads with swarms of our people. Refugees from the frontier districts and more than 80,000 construction workers from the fortified areas were heading toward the interior of the country. Workers, the families of soldiers, and many collective farmers had been forced to leave their homes without notice. Most of them had

---

[2] Defense zones between the border and Leningrad which were heavily planted with antitank barriers.—Ed.

not the time to take along outer clothing. Enemy bombs and machine-gun fire killed large numbers of adults and children on the roads.

After occupying Lithuania and Latvia in a few days, Von Leeb's forces crossed the frontier of the Russian Soviet Federated Socialist Republic. Advanced motorized units drove toward Pskov. Enemy ground operations were actively supported by the 1,070 combat aircraft of the German First Air Force. In the north, seven Finnish infantry divisions advanced on Leningrad across the Karelian Isthmus.

On July 10 enemy armored units broke through the Eleventh Army front south of Pskov and rolled in a wide stream toward Luga. Leningrad was 180–200 kilometers away. At the rate they were advancing, the Germans would need nine or ten days to reach the outskirts of the city. Enemy forces were still far superior to those of our Northwestern Front on July 10. Leeb commanded twenty-three divisions, totaling 340,000 officers and men. He had more than six thousand artillery pieces and mortars, 326 tanks, and about one thousand airplanes. There were not more than 150,000 Soviet fighting men facing the enemy. Good defensive positions in the rear did not yet exist. Construction of the defense line at Luga was far from complete. The situation was extremely dangerous and difficult.

On July 11, at the height of the battle, the commander-in-chief of the Northwestern Front, Marshal of the Soviet Union K. E. Voroshilov, arrived in Leningrad on orders of the government of the USSR. He understood the unfavorable situation which was developing at the front. At the same time he knew the spirit of the Soviet people, who would prefer mortal combat to cowardice.

Pinning their hopes on unity and the great desire to smash the enemy, and with the active assistance of the Leningrad party, Soviet headquarters turned every means at its disposal to resist the advancing enemy. Human and material resources were mobilized both to repulse German attacks and to build additional defense positions on the approaches to Leningrad. Brigades of marines were hastily formed from the personnel of ships, naval units, and academies, with more than eighty thousand men from the Baltic

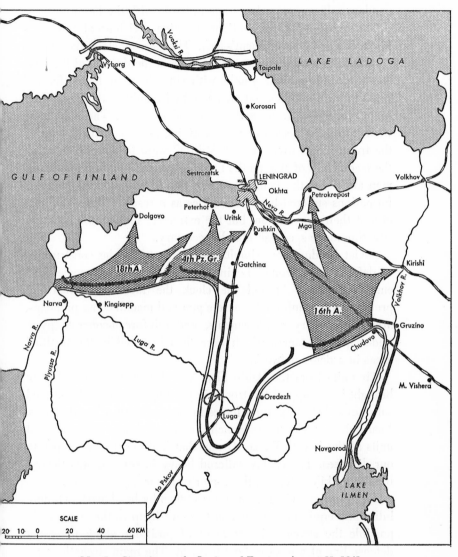

MAP 1.—Situation on the Leningrad Front on August 21, 1941

Fleet being sent into action on land. These marines displayed exemplary selflessness and courage in battle with the Fascists.

The people of Leningrad formed nine divisions of "People's Militia" at the government's call. The personnel of these divisions, which played an outstanding role in the defense of the city, was extremely varied: youths with rifles in their hands for the first time and middle-aged men who had fought in the Civil War; some physically strong and hardy; others puny. The volunteers went through a period of hasty training and were hurried off to the front. Three divisions of "Militia" were fighting as early as the second half of July on the Luga defense line and repulsed German attacks at the Ivanovskoe and Sabsk bridgeheads. The new formations suffered heavy casualties as a result of the inadequacies of their preparation, but the extremely unfavorable military situation made speed absolutely necessary.

Soviet headquarters simultaneously hastened the construction of defense belts around Leningrad. Up to 500,000 people were employed daily. Around the clock the factories turned out prefabricated reinforced-concrete gun and machine-gun pillboxes, armored artillery emplacements, and reinforced-concrete pyramid-shaped obstacles, which were then installed in the fortified areas in a dense network.

Air units from the Baltic Fleet and the Northern Front were brought in to support the troops in the Luga sector and rendered substantial help to ground forces in actions against hostile tanks. Near Soltsy, Soviet forces launched a daring counterstroke against units of the Fourth Panzer Group that had penetrated deep into our defenses. The enemy suffered heavy losses and was thrown back forty kilometers on this sector of the front.

The rapid and vigorous measures taken by headquarters to mobilize and equip manpower and to move it up to the front made possible the strong reinforcement of positions along the Luga defense line at a most critical moment. The main strength of resistance to the enemy lay not in our positions, however (they were hurriedly constructed and did not constitute real obstacles to tanks), but in the tenacity and staunchness of the soldiers and the courageous behavior of their officers. It was the spirit of self-

less bravery among our fighting men which was the invincible force in the resistance.

The headlong attacks of the Germans and their extraordinary attempts to smash forward came to nothing. Disabled tanks and vast numbers of dead lay scattered over a wide expanse of territory. His heavy losses finally forced the enemy to go over to the defensive. Feverishly, Leeb began to consolidate the overextended elements of his armies and move up his combat supply train. When substantial forces had been concentrated and regrouped, the Germans launched an offensive on August 8–10, with strong air support from dive bombers especially. Although a success was achieved in breaching our defenses and enemy spearheads were moving again toward Leningrad, the tempo of the enemy advance was no longer what it had been in the first days of the war. Resistance increased daily. If up to July 10 the Germans advanced with an average speed of twenty-six kilometers per day, the tempo of their advance during the rest of July was reduced more than five times over: it did not exceed five kilometers. In August, it did not exceed 2.2 kilometers per day, and every kilometer of the route was covered with the corpses of Fascist soldiers. The enemy army was still powerful, however. He controlled the air and punished our ground forces severely. In pushing Soviet forces back, the Fascist troops were each day approaching a cherished goal. Fires lit their way; gusts of wind carried ashes and smoke to the suburbs of Leningrad. Sick at heart, and in deep sorrow, the populace evacuated workers' settlements, towns, and villages, destroying crops and driving off the cattle. The refugees moved east along many roads and highways; most of them went no farther than Leningrad.

To a meeting of the Leningrad party activists on August 20 Voroshilov reported the situation at the front. He indicated on a map the dispositions of the enemy and of our own troops. The front line was broken. In the area of Krasnogvardeisk (Gatchina) the enemy was already quite close to Leningrad. The whole German striking force had now been concentrated at the front. Voroshilov and A. A. Zhdanov called the attention of the

7

activists to this fact. The Communists listened intently to every word about headquarters' plans for fighting the enemy. "As you see," said Voroshilov, "the situation is difficult, but we have the capability not only to halt the enemy's advance, but to smash and destroy him. Bear in mind that the enemy will carry out a savage attack, that he will use both aviation and artillery. Now we've got enough artillery to give him as good as we get and then some. We must produce more shells, mines, mortars. We'll not only not let the enemy inside Leningrad, we'll beat him here. Leningrad will become his grave."

Speaking at the same meeting, Zhdanov said:

> The moment has come to put your Bolshevik qualities to work, to get ready to defend Leningrad without wasting words. We must organize close co-operation between the approaches to the city and the city itself. What we have to do is teach people in the shortest possible time the main and most important methods of combat: shooting, throwing grenades, street fighting, digging trenches, crawling. We must sign up the young people for auxiliary work in labor battalions: they can carry shells, water, act as messengers, and so on. We have to see that nobody is just an onlooker, and carry out in the least possible time the same kind of mobilization of the workers of Leningrad that was done in 1918 and 1919. We have to fight tendencies toward inefficiency and complacency in ourselves. The enemy is at the gates. It is a question of life or death. Either the working class of Leningrad will be enslaved and its finest flower destroyed, or we must gather all the strength we have, hit back twice as hard, and dig Fascism a grave in front of Leningrad. All depends on us. Let's be strong, organized, powerful, and victory will be ours.[3]

On the morning of August 21 the attention of the city's population was riveted upon a manifesto to the people issued by the Northwestern Front Military Council, the Leningrad Party Committee, and the Leningrad Soviet of Workers' Deputies. The man-

[3] The words of K. E. Voroshilov and A. A. Zhdanov are quoted from notes made by the author.

8

ifesto was short and expressive; it reflected the real situation and the popular mood:

Comrades, Leningraders, Dear Friends!

Over our beloved native city hangs the immediate threat of attack by German-Fascist troops. The enemy is trying to penetrate to Leningrad. He wants to destroy our homes, to seize our factories and plants, to drench our streets and squares with the blood of innocent victims, to outrage our peaceful population, to enslave the free sons of our Motherland. But this shall not be. Leningrad—cradle of the proletarian revolution, mighty industrial and cultural center of our country—never was and never will be in enemy hands. We have not lived and worked in our beautiful city, we have not built with our own hands the great factories and plants of Leningrad, its splendid buildings and gardens, to have it all fall to the German-Fascist bandits.

Never shall this be. . . .

Let us rise like one man to the defense of our city, our homes, our families, our honor, and freedom. Let us perform our sacred duty as Soviet patriots and be indomitable in the struggle with the fierce and hateful enemy, vigilant and merciless in the struggle with cowards, alarmists, and deserters; let us establish the strictest revolutionary order in our city. Armed with iron discipline and Bolshevik efficiency we shall meet the enemy bravely and give him a crushing repulse.

A new flood of strength was evoked from men's hearts by the appeal; it aroused fury and anger against the enemy, and it suppressed alarm and bitterness of heart at the news of the Fascists' proximity to Leningrad. Like an alarm bell in the night, the appeal summoned everyone to defend his city, his family, his honor, and freedom. Men, women, and youngsters hurried to the posts to which their leaders sent them, fully resolved to defend the city at any cost.

It is to the great honor of the organizers of Leningrad's defense that they assigned hundreds of thousands of people quickly and skilfully to the variety of tasks on which the defense depended. Some went to join the People's Militia or the partisan detachments, some to build defense lines, and some to care for the wounded in the hospitals. Others went to factories and plants producing more weapons or clothing for the soldiers. No one stood aside. Every inhabitant burned with the holy fire of hatred for invaders. The common will of a population of three million created a force that could not be crushed.

The party organization gave special attention to selecting the personnel for partisan warfare. They had to be physically strong and determined. The Military Council dispatched to the rear of the hostile army several of these partisan detachments, and each one numbered upward of one thousand men. As he gave instruction to the partisan commanders, Voroshilov would say:

> The enemy is bold and shameless; he is counting on our inefficiency; he is moving forward in small groups, without reconnaissance; he thinks nobody likes the Soviet system and there's no one to be afraid of; he takes few precautionary measures and we must exploit this. We don't have much strength; it will take some time for us to get strong. The enemy must be halted by blows at his rear, along his communications, delivered mostly at night. We have to hit this overweening enemy hard from behind. Your detachments will have losses, but the enemy will lose ten times more. The population will support you in this noble work.

Events showed that such mobile partisan detachments gave invaluable help to the troops of the Leningrad Front. Roads were mined and bridges along the routes of the Fascist troops were blown up, the German-Fascist army suffering heavy losses from the sabotage.

The *raion*[4] committees of the party established a constant watch over the most important industrial enterprises to keep them running without interruption. Among the factories themselves there was maximum liaison and co-operation to assure a high level of productivity. Plants and factories turning out consumer goods switched over two-thirds of their capacity to produce ammunition, signal equipment, electronic equipment, and other tools of war.

Also in answer to the call, as in July, everyone able to work

[4] The city party organization was divided into neighborhood, or *raion*, sections. *Oblast* is an administrative designation of a larger area; e.g., Leningrad *oblast*.

went out to build defensive positions around Leningrad and a second defense belt along the line Gulf of Finland–Settlement No. 3–Predportovaya Station–Circle Railroad–Novaya Derevnya–Staraya Derevnya–Gulf of Finland. The whole zone was divided into seven sectors. In the inner defense belt, as on the approaches to the city, antitank ditches were dug as well as full-size fire trenches and a well-developed system of communication trenches. The fortified areas were armed with artillery, including naval guns, both ashore and on board ships. Each gun and battery was assigned its field of fire in advance.

The work of constructing the defense belts was directed by a commission of seven men, headed by A. A. Kuznetsov, a member of the Military Council and secretary of the Leningrad Party Committee. The commission had the right to mobilize men and material resources and to enrol scientists and specialists for necessary work in building the fortifications.

Endowed with unusual capacity for work, Kuznetsov would set about any assigned task with zeal and optimism. Now too he put the whole force of his fiery nature and youthful fervor into organizing the masses to build the defensive rampart girdling the city; the days that would decide the fate of the defense were numbered. Much of his time Kuznetsov spent at the construction sites, trying to understand the details of unfamiliar structures, tirelessly checking deliveries of materials for building the great belts of fortifications. Well acquainted with many of the directors, engineers, and technical experts, as well as with the productive capabilities of the major factories, he enlisted the services of these men, depending on their knowledge and experience to produce what was needed for this unusual construction. Stalin more than once gave Kuznetsov direct instructions on building the fortified belts and preparing the population for the defense of the city. It must be said, too, that Kuznetsov carried them out ably and quickly. His constant good humor, despite difficulties, attracted men of various professions to him; they trusted him and readily performed tasks he assigned. The quick, energetic, and well-thought-out measures taken by the Leningraders insured that the fortified belts were constructed with a high degree of modern engineering skill, a fact that played an important part in the defense of Leningrad.

In April, 1920, V. I. Lenin said:

Every time a difficult situation occurred in the war, the party mobilized the Communists and they were the first to die, in the front ranks. They died by thousands against Yudenich and Kolchak; the best of the working class died, sacrificed themselves, knowing they would die but would save those to come, would save thousands and thousands of workers and peasants.[5]

This time, too, the party was on guard. Seventy per cent of the Leningrad party membership and 90 per cent of the Comsomols took up arms. Communists and Comsomols led the way to death. They displayed great heroism in barring the road to the enemy. The motherland and the freedom won by the blood of the workers were in danger, and, at the party's call, the people rose as one to defend their native land. Love for the motherland has always exerted a great attraction, but it showed with special force during the war with the Fascist invaders.

Knowing the usefulness and necessity of their work, hundreds of thousands of people worked tirelessly everywhere—on the approaches of the city, in the plants and factories, on the streets and in the squares. With faith in victory, they were zealously transforming the city into a fortress. Townspeople and collective farmers from the surrounding districts worked without pause to build the fortified lines. In a short time, they completed a girdle of anti-tank ditches 626 kilometers long, built 15,000 reinforced concrete firing points and trenches, and thirty-five kilometers of barricades. As the thunder of artillery came nearer, it spurred the defenders on to finish what they had begun rather than frightening them.

The soldiers and the people were not prepared to let the enemy into Leningrad. If the foe nevertheless managed to break into the city, a plan had been worked out in detail for destroying his troops. Factories, bridges, and public buildings were mined and would have been blown up at signal; stone and iron wreckage

[5] V. I. Lenin, *Works* (35 vols.; Leningrad, 1941–50), XXX, 464. Reference is to the Russian edition.

would have crashed down upon the heads of enemy soldiers and halted their tanks. The civilian population, not to mention the soldiers and sailors, was prepared to fight in the streets. The idea of a house-by-house fight did not simply mean self-sacrifice; its object was to destroy the enemy. As the experience of Stalingrad later confirmed, the stubborn resistance of a great city can lead to the defeat of a powerful enemy force.

August was a month of extreme tension, especially for those who bore the full responsibility of military operations. During these hot days the men at headquarters hardly closed their eyes. Heavy fighting was taking place on the nearest approaches to Leningrad. Everyone who had a weapon was thrown into the battle. As never before, a firm and constant direction of military operations was required. At the same time the danger of any enemy penetration into the city forced the leadership to spend much of its time implementing the defense plans for the city. On August 20 the Northwestern Sector Military Council, in order to strengthen its defensive measures, formed a "Leningrad Defense Military Council" and assigned it responsibility for directing the work of building defense lines around and inside the city, training the adult population in basic methods of combat, increasing the output of arms and ammunition for the front and the workers' battalions, and a variety of other functions.

But this plan for a Military Council was soon changed.

Comrades Voroshilov and Zhdanov were called to the telephone to talk to Supreme Headquarters on August 21. Stalin expressed dissatisfaction that they had created a city defense council without his permission and considered it incorrect, once it had been formed, that Voroshilov and Zhdanov were not members. Voroshilov and Zhdanov explained that the City Defense Military Council had been formed to meet the needs of the actual situation, that it was an auxiliary body for performing certain defense tasks that would relieve the extremely overburdened Northwestern Sector Military Council, and that they had decided not to be members in order to have more time to direct the military operations on whose outcome the fate of Leningrad depended. Stalin rejected their arguments and suggested that they review the membership of the Defense Council. His instructions were followed at once. Voroshilov became the head of the Leningrad Defense Military Council, and Zhdanov, Kuznetsov, Subbotin, and Popkov became members. Thus during the fiercest days of fighting between great armies two councils were created headed essentially by the same individuals. From the technical standpoint of unity of command, the order may have been correct. In practice, however, the functions of the Sector Military Council were confused with those of the Leningrad Defense Military Council; the commander-in-chief was deluged with problems that could have been dealt with by other competent people. As things turned out, the activities of this unsuccessfully organized council lasted no more than six days.

Taking into account developments in the Northwestern Sector —specifically the occupation of the northern shore of Lake Ladoga by the Finns, which made it impossible to command Soviet troops from Ladoga to Murmansk from headquarters in Leningrad—the State Defense Committee decided on August 23 to divide the Northern Front into two: the Karelian Front and the Leningrad Front, and to subordinate the Northwestern Front directly to the Supreme Command. In connection with this the Leningrad Defense Military Council was dissolved on August 30, and all its duties were transferred to the Leningrad Front Military Council. These decisions of the State Defense Committee had very great significance because front commanders (Karelian, Leningrad, Northwestern) could now direct military operations on shorter sections, thus enabling them to give more attention to the operations of individual formations and units; and it was now possible to devise a more efficient system for directing the defense of Leningrad.

The German divisions, meanwhile, exploiting their superior strength, pushed deeper and deeper into the country. On August 21 hostile forces occupied the station of Chudovo, cutting the October railroad; eight days later they took Tosno, advancing on Mga Station, Yam-Izhora, and Ivanovskoe. After stubborn fighting the German Thirty-ninth Motorized Corps captured Mga, an important railroad junction. Leningrad's last railroad connection with the rest of the country had been cut.

To break through the defense and take the city by storm, the German-Fascist command had brought into the action more than a thousand tanks, about one thousand aircraft, and great quantities of mortars and artillery: the enemy had five or six times as much matériel as the Soviet forces. Enveloping Leningrad from all sides, the Germans launched concentric attacks from the south, southwest, and north. Elements of the German Sixteenth Army achieved the greatest success; they began to envelop the city from the east, pushing forward along the left bank of the Neva toward Lake Ladoga. On the morning of September 6 about three hundred German bombers attacked a narrow section of the front where troops of the NKVD First Division were defending the approaches to Schluesselburg. Air attacks by the Germans lasted all day, as one wave of bombers succeeded another; the division lost heavily in men and matériel. Despite great heroism on the part of Soviet fliers in combat with the enemy air force, the situation in this section of the front remained unfavorable. Our aviation was still numerically inferior. The heavy losses sustained in surprise enemy attacks during the first days continued seriously to hamper military operations. After the air attacks, the enemy threw armored units into the battle for Schluesselberg.

The soldiers of the Soviet Army offered stubborn resistance to the enemy. As quickly as hostile aircraft departed, our units launched counterattacks, throwing back the German infantry and tanks. Next morning German air raids and tank attacks intensified. Enemy aircraft were overhead at all times. Under the pressure of superior enemy forces the Soviet troops began to retreat. By 11:00 A.M. on September 8 German armor had split retreating units of the First Division in two. One group, in heavy fighting, got across to the right bank of the Neva; the other retreated to the east. The Fascists reached the southern shores of Lake Ladoga and took Schluesselburg, a city located at the sources of the Neva. The flag of our motherland, however, continued to wave over the citadel of this city for a long time, when a small Soviet garrison held out. They inflicted heavy losses on the enemy.

Leningrad was thus blockaded on land beginning September 8. At the same time the movement of ships from Lake Ladoga down the Neva was paralyzed. During the night of September 8–9, the enemy tried to cross the wide, deep Neva on rafts in the Porogi-Sheremetievka sector but abandoned the attempt after suffering large losses from the fire of workers' detachments guarding the right bank. This natural defense line proved a reliable shield for the besieged under cover of which they confidently beat off enemy attacks.

Attempts by enemy forces to break through to Leningrad from the south were unsuccessful. On August 21 our units were still holding their defense lines in the vicinity of Luga. As a result of the appearance of the enemy at Gatchina to the west, however, and the advance of the German Sixteenth Army via Chudovo to Kolpino, Soviet forces in the Luga area were now in an extremely difficult position. Threatened with complete encirclement, they were compelled to retreat north in heavy fighting. (See Map 1.) On September 12 the Germans took Krasnoe Selo and Slutsk. Despite numerous casualties they continued to move forward and on September 17 reached the southern coast of the Gulf of Finland.

In the north, advancing Finnish troops occupied Beloostrov on September 4 but were driven out of the town next day. The enemy took Olonets on September 5; two days later the Finns reached the Svir River. They succeeded in crossing the river after stubborn fighting and on September 12 took Podporozhe. The giant pincers that had grasped for Leningrad were tightening. If the forward units of the German army, pushing up from the south, could cover a little more ground, they would make contact with the Finns. The nearness of the goal gave enemy forces the strength and the tenacity for furious attacks upon the Soviet defense lines. Fascist propaganda aroused the offensive spirit in their soldiers and spread the word that governmental institutions, factories, and the population were being evacuated from Leningrad and that against the attacks of German troops and their Finnish allies the city would not hold out even a few days.

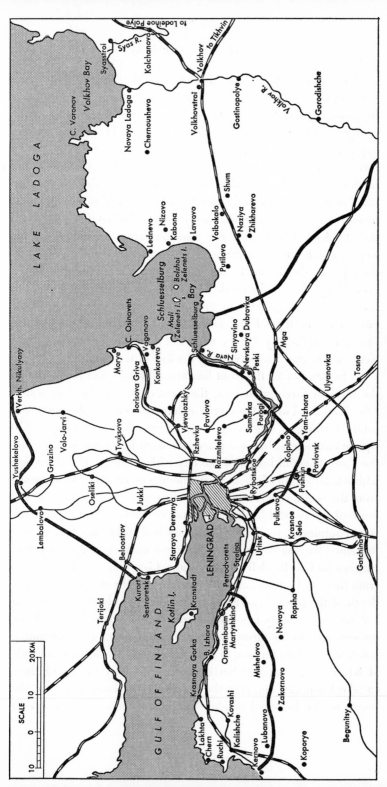

MAP 2.—Soviet front line at Leningrad on September 21, 1941

Leningrad was now going through terrible days. Artillery bombardments of the city, air raids, and fires became more frequent. These forerunners of the advancing Fascist army brought about a general increase in tension. The Germans were applying pressure from all sides but concentrated their largest forces of tanks and artillery on the approaches to Uritsk and in the area of the Pulkovo Heights. Their assaults on the fortified lines went on with brief intermissions until the end of September. Supported by tanks, enemy soldiers hurled themselves into the attacks but each time ran into murderous fire from the besieged which cut them down in great numbers and burned out their tanks. Resistance to the enemy increased as hostile forces grew daily more exhausted. The Germans failed, moreover, to take the Pulkovo Heights, an area which dominated a considerable part of the battlefield and permitted observation of the defense lines around the city. On the northeast the Finns grew weaker and went over to the defensive along the line of the Svir.

By September 29 the front line around Leningrad had assumed the form of three great arcs, their extremities resting on water. (See Map 2.) Two of these arcs inclosed the city on the north and south, forming a large ring with an area inside totaling 2,850 square kilometers. In some places the front line came so near that the Fascists could bombard the city with artillery. The third arc, with a total length of about sixty kilometers, covered the sea coast from the south, squeezing the defending units against the sea. Defense of the coastal bridgehead was extremely difficult. Ammunition, equipment, food, and medicines had to be supplied by sea, but since the sea route along the coast came under enemy fire, cargoes had to be delivered to Cape Lisy Nos and transported from there to Oranienbaum by sea to avoid the danger zone. The depth of the bridgehead at its widest place (Lubanovo–Chernaya Lakhta) was twenty-five kilometers. The Germans launched numerous attacks to throw the Soviet units from this remaining patch of land into the sea, to seize the Baltic Fleet's powerful forts at Krasnaya Gorka and Seriya Loshad, and by means of them to take Kronstadt and turn the muzzles of its cannon against the breast of the besieged citadel. The staunchness and courage of

18

sailors and soldiers enabled them to hold the little patch of land vital to the defense of the city. (The bridgehead played an important part when our troops smashed the enemy in 1944.)

The enemy spearhead that reached the Gulf of Finland captured a strip of coast twenty kilometers long from Peterhof to the southwestern outskirts of Leningrad and did considerable damage to the defenders, especially the troops in the coastal bridgehead. The Fascist troops in this area then found that they themselves were in poor position. They suffered severe losses from the heavy fire of warships and the long-range guns of the forts.

When convinced of the fruitlessness of further attacks, headquarters of the Supreme Command of Hitler's forces issued a special directive:

Fuehrer's GHQ, 7/10/41
Supreme Command of the Wehrmacht
No. 41 1675/41 Secret Chancery, *Wehrmachtsfuehrungstab/*
Section L (1 ops.)

To: Supreme Command of the Army (Operations Section)
The Fuehrer has decided once more that a surrender on the part of Leningrad, or later of Moscow, will not be accepted even if offered by the enemy.

The moral justification for this decision is clear for all the world to see. If in Kiev very grave dangers were created for our troops by delayed action explosions, this must be expected to an even greater extent in Moscow and Leningrad. The Soviet radio itself has announced that Leningrad has been mined and will be defended to the last man.

Serious danger of plagues is to be expected.

No German soldiers therefore are to enter these cities. Whoever tries to approach our lines from the city will be turned back by fire. Flight of the population into interior Russia through minor unsealed gaps in our lines is to be encouraged. All other cities too are to be worn down before capture by artillery fire and air attacks, and their population caused to flee.

There can be no reason for exposing the lives of German soldiers to enemy fire in order to save Russian cities or to

feed their populations at the expense of the German home-
land.

The chaos in Russia will become all the greater, our
administration and exploitation of the occupied eastern
provinces will be that much easier, the more the populations of Soviet-Russian cities escape into the interior of
Russia.

The Fuehrer's will is to be brought to the attention of all
commanding officers.

For the Chief of Staff of the Supreme Command of the
Wehrmacht:

Signed: Jodl[6]

Aside from its utter cynicism, it is a feature of this directive
that Hitler and his staff admitted their inability to take Leningrad by storm. At the same time, Hitler could not give up the
thought of capturing the city. His commanders were now being
told to change their tactics: instead of making an assault, they
were to commence a siege, to destroy the city by air bombardment
and artillery fire, and the city's population with it.

By the end of September, 1941, Leeb's army had advanced
about nine hundred kilometers into the northwestern part of the
Soviet Union. Having already seized the Baltic provinces, Pskov,
Novgorod, much of the Leningrad *oblast,* and important naval
bases on the Baltic Sea, the Fascist troops now hovered like a
black cloud over Leningrad. The city and the troops of the Leningrad Front were within an encircling ring, while the Baltic Fleet was
squeezed into a corner of the Gulf of Finland. Delivery of supplies for the population of the great city, the troops of the Front,
and the Fleet from other areas of the country virtually ceased.
Only a narrow water lane across Lake Ladoga had not yet been
cut off by the enemy, but even this route was exposed to enemy
fire and air attacks. All this gave the Fascist army reason to hold
its head high and count on speedy victory.

[6] Jodl, the signatory of the document, was hanged five years later as
a war criminal. [The given English version of the document has been
translated from the original German.—Ed.]

There was another aspect to these successes of Hitler's army, however. The capture of a considerable amount of territory had not been consolidated by a strategic success. Leningrad remained in Soviet hands and thereby pinned down around the city a hostile army of more than 300,000 men. The land that had been temporarily conquered, from the Niemen to the Neva, was plentifully watered with blood; the road of victories had become a road of graves. As of September 25, 1941, more than 190,000 German officers and men had been killed or wounded, five hundred guns and seven hundred tanks had been lost. The line of communications connecting East Prussia with the combat troops was very much extended. The Soviet population in the territory occupied by the enemy was under constant surveillance by the unsleeping eye of the Gestapo and other Nazi agencies but men and women nevertheless hit the Fascist army from behind as hard as they could. The partisans were very active. And ahead—winter. . . .

Even though they had sustained heavy casualties and were caught in the vise of blockade, the troops of the Leningrad Front had not been defeated; they were, on the contrary, like a compressed spring and were becoming more dangerous and threatening.

This first and most acute period of the battle for Leningrad had not brought Fascist Germany the desired results; her objective had not been attained and time had been irrevocably lost. Hitler was aware of this very unpleasant aspect of his successes. His initial good humor changed to dissatisfaction and alarm. The causes of the failure of the rapidly moving operations he saw in the individuals who were carrying out these plans, not in the mistakes and miscalculations inherent in his own strategic plans. Natures like Hitler's, completely autocratic and egotistical, seldom see people and their actions in the light of reality; it usually seems to them that everything around ought to happen as they wish it. If life does not turn out as they hope, it must be as a result of the intrigues of people who cannot or will not fulfil their wishes.

Hitler summoned prominent generals to the Reich Chancellory and expounded his views on events at Leningrad. Striding excitedly up and down his office, he shouted nervously: "Leeb is in second childhood; he can't grasp and carry out my plan for the speedy capture of Leningrad. He fusses over his plan of assuming the defensive in the northwestern sector and wants a drive in the center on Moscow. He's obviously senile, he's lost his nerve, and like a true Catholic he wants to pray but not fight." No one present interrupted the enraged Fuehrer; they "yessed" him and praised his "far-sighted" plans. In December, 1941, Leeb was removed from command of Army Group North. But to avoid undesirable comment at home and abroad and to forestall suspicions that all was not well at the front, it was announced officially that Von Leeb had been relieved at his own request, on grounds of temporary illness, and that Hitler greatly regretted this and hoped for the Field Marshal's speedy convalescence. And so Von Leeb, who had been praised to the skies, promoted to Field Marshal, and decorated with the Knight's Cross for his victory in the west, disappeared from the political scene after five months of war on the eastern front.

Hitler made Colonel General Kuechler commander of Army Group North, a man who served fascism with enthusiasm. In May, 1940, under Kuechler's command, the German Eighteenth Army had invaded neutral Holland, and, breaking the resistance of the small but brave Dutch army, had advanced into Belgium. Defeating the Belgian armed forces and taking Antwerp, the Eighteenth Army, with other German armies, invaded France where Kuechler finished the war by bringing his forces to the Pas de Calais coast near Dunkirk. Kuechler was promoted to colonel general for his performance in the French campaign. Hitler hoped the new commander of Army Group North would make good the deficiencies of his ill-starred predecessor.

But though Kuechler commanded there more than two years, from December, 1941, through January, 1944, he could neither alter the situation at Leningrad nor advance a single step toward victory. To maintain the blockade he sank ships bringing food to the city, dropped parachute mines of great explosive force, and bombarded the city at long range with heavy caliber shells, having no idea where they might fall. Everything he did showed his intention to terrorize the population. The tyrant resorted to every kind of cunning and cruel device. In all military history it would be hard to find a general who destroyed more civilians than Kuechler did. On June 30, 1942, in a special order, Hitler noted his "lofty" services to the Fascist empire and promoted him to the rank of Field Marshal, which did not, however, prevent Hitler from immediately removing Kuechler from his post and retiring him when Soviet troops in January, 1944, had fully relieved the blockade of Leningrad.[7]

The German propaganda machine, headed by Hitler's fanatically devoted servant Goebbels, did not mention the collapse of the High Command's strategic plans and continued to sing the praises of Hitler's genius as a commander, predicting the imminent fall of encircled Leningrad. It is clear, however, that encirclement is not victory. Fascist propaganda foretold the end of the story imprudently and in doing so went too far.

Hitler's headquarters now pinned its hopes on the successful conduct of a siege—on encircling the city with a double ring in order to starve it out. The distance between the right flank of the Finnish troops on the Svir River and German units east of Mga was 120–130 kilometers. To exert pressure on the defenders, the command of Army Group North decided to undertake a deep envelopment of Leningrad from the east, selecting for this purpose the Thirty-ninth Motorized Corps, which was assigned a large number of tanks. The corps commander, General Schmidt, was ordered to seal off access to the city by way of Lake Ladoga, to make contact with the Finns on the Svir River, to take Tikhvin, and advance on Vologda, severing the communications of the Karelian Front.

At the beginning of October the battle became an acute struggle for control of lines of communication: on the German side, to cut the last artery by which the besieged population could be fed; on the Soviet side, to break through the blockade and regain control of the lost routes.

[7] At the end of the war Kuechler was arrested by American occupation authorities. He was tried in 1948 by a military court which found him guilty of crimes against humanity and sentenced him to twenty years imprisonment. In 1953, however, this convicted criminal was released, allegedly on account of illness and old age. Kuechler thus spent only eight years in prison.

2

THE BEGINNING OF THE SIEGE

September–December, 1941

AFTER THE DECISION against storming the city, the enemy dug in and constructed solid defense positions around Leningrad. The sector Mga-Sinyavino was fortified with particular thoroughness— the small area was filled with artillery, mortars, reinforced-concrete firing points, and a thick network of barbed-wire obstacles— because it was feared that this was where Soviet forces might attempt to break through. Here only a narrow strip about sixteen kilometers wide separated the Soviet Fifty-fourth Army from the troops of the Neva Group inside the ring. The Germans' fear was shortly justified, for Soviet troops launched an attack on the Mga-Sinyavino sector from the east, with the objective of breaking the blockade and linking up with the defenders of Leningrad. But opportunity had been lost; the Germans had had time to fortify themselves too well. All the violent attacks of our troops were beaten off, and it would yet require sixteen long months of bloody struggle to smash enemy resistance and break the blockade.

The enemy brought up long-range artillery and on September 1, the beginning of the long ordeal of Leningrad, the first shells were fired at the city from 240 millimeter guns. The bombardment consisted of single rounds from the direction of Tosno. Shells struck the Bolshevik Works, the Salolin Works, and Hydroelectric Station No. 5. A fire was started in the hydrogen shop at the Salolin Works. The first shell bursts in the streets came as a surprise. The people had known that the enemy was getting close, but somehow it was unbelievable that he was close enough to fire on the city. People could not adjust to the calamity for a long time. During the first three days of artillery fire, 53 people were killed and 101 wounded. Soon the enemy also commenced an intensive air bombardment of the city, dropping hundreds of incendiary and high-explosive bombs. Fires were started, and the piercing shrieks of sirens split the air frequently.

On September 8, at 6:55 in the evening, enemy aircraft carried out a violent attack on the city, dropping 6,327 incendiary bombs. Five thousand fell in the Moskovsky *raion*, 1,311 in the Smolninsky, and sixteen in the Krasnogvardeisky *raions*. The bombs contained napalm, a highly combustible jelly-like substance. The compound caught fire instantly. Such bombs were very hard to extinguish. One hundred seventy-eight fires broke out in various *raions*, in industrial plants, dwelling places, and commercial warehouses. Houses, streets, bridges, people, hidden by darkness, would suddenly be lit up by the ominous flames of vast conflagrations. Thick black puffs of smoke mounted slowly into the sky, poisoning the air with the smell of burning. Night was coming on, and it seemed that nothing could stop the advancing sea of flames. Firemen, civil defense groups, and thousands of workers, despite the weariness after a day's work, threw themselves into the battle with the fire and only by frantic efforts brought the flames under control and then put them out altogether. The fire at the Badaev warehouses, however, raged more than five hours.

On the same day, at 10:35 P.M., heavy bombers dropped forty-eight high-explosive bombs ranging in weight from 250 to 500 kilograms. Most of them fell near Smolny Institute and the Finland Station. Twelve dwelling places were destroyed by direct hits, the pumping plant at the city waterworks was severely damaged, as was the House of Peasants, located one hundred meters from the main building of Smolny Institute. Twenty-four people died under the debris of houses that night and 122 were wounded. The local civil defense met the second attack more effectively. Anti-aircraft gunners shot down five aircraft; unexploded bombs were disarmed and the streets cleared.

On September 9, and with greater force on the tenth, the enemy continued his air attacks on the city. From an altitude of six thousand meters the Germans dropped 69 bombs of great explosive force and 1,794 incendiary bombs. Some of the incendiaries had small explosives attached to them which burst when the incendiary device had finished burning. Some of the incendiaries weighed as much as 50 kilograms. Twenty-eight major fires and 55 lesser ones were started; 84 people were killed during these two days and 622 were wounded. Once again many incendiary bombs fell on the Badaev warehouses; this time three wooden warehouses burned down. One of these contained spare parts for machinery but two were empty.[1] From the first days of September on, the city was subjected to constant air attacks which caused considerable loss of life and destruction of property.

The German fighter pilots hurled themselves furiously at the Soviet "Sea-gull" fighters, making good advantage of the superior speed of their Messerschmitts. The battles in the air were fierce; Soviet fliers resorted to ramming when they ran out of ammunition. Airmen like Pyotr Kharitonov, Mikhail Zhukov, Stepan Zdorovtsev, and others, whose ramming attacks brought enemy bombers crashing into the ground, are remembered by the people of Leningrad.

Soon after the first raids the enemy began to drop delayed-action bombs in great quantities on the city. This was, of course, a deliberate attempt by the enemy to deprive the besieged population of the use of large sections of the city's transit lines for prolonged periods of time, to stop work at the most important plants, to paralyze the industrial activity of the inhabitants of entire *raions,* and to spread panic among the people. Because it was not then known how to disarm the bombs and because the enemy used detonators of different types and designs, the delayed-action explosives were a real danger. This was a problem that had to be solved quickly, for the unexploded bombs had the potential to do immense harm to the defense of the city.

At that time the technique of disposing of a delayed-action

---

[1] Details of the effects of the raids on September 8, 9, and 10 are taken from the Military Council's reports to Supreme Headquarters on September 9 and 12, 1941. One kilogram equals 2.2046 lb.—Ed.

bomb had not been perfected: the bomb was dug out with spades and Civil Defense personnel then climbed into the hole to tame the shrew, which might explode at any moment. Since the bomb might go off while it was being dismantled, the work of disarming was performed by a single individual. The method of disarming such bombs was decided upon at the spot where it fell and with regard to the particular situation. In order to eliminate the danger of explosion as quickly as possible, it was often the practice to knock off the clamp ring of the detonator with a hammer instead of unscrewing it with a socket wrench. Fifteen or twenty minutes would pass and the deadly threat would be eliminated. But what minutes! How much strength and nervous tension they demanded of the people who performed this fearful but noble work! And there were cases when bombs went off and blew those working on them to bits. Nevertheless there were many volunteers specifically for this work, who fearlessly carried on the heroic work of their fallen comrades. Squads of volunteers were formed in all the *raions*. These were resolute, courageous people. We often use the word "courageous" when speaking of the Leningraders and their struggle during the blockade, and this is proper. Only people endowed with great strength of heart could have accomplished what they did. But the word applies most of all to the members of the bomb-disposal squads. There were many girls from the Comsomol among the volunteers in these squads, and some of them disarmed twenty or thirty bombs. Every time you watched a duel between one of them and a heavy bomb, it would seem that the young patriot could not have time or strength enough to open the iron casing and disarm the bomb. But they did have the strength. During these years of severe trials, the members of the Leningrad Comsomol showed what they could do in the name of the motherland.

A bomb fell on the streetcar depot on Serdobolsky Street. Smashing down through ceilings and floors, it landed in the cellar and did not explode. Everyone was immediately evacuated from the danger zone, which was cordoned off, and *raion* headquarters of Civil Defense was informed. A platoon commander from one of the C.D. detachments soon arrived: a slim young girl with lively

27

black eyes, Anna Nikolaevna Kovaleva, who had not yet actually disarmed a bomb. After surveying the hole in the floor to determine the approximate size of the bomb, she lit a candle and boldly crawled down into the cellar to carry out her terrifying assignment.

The flickering light of the candle in the dark cellar revealed rows of posts, 0.6 of a meter in height, over which ran water pipes and electric cables stretching away into the distance. Somewhere in the dark, damp cellar, filled with the monotonous hum of the cables, the monster was lurking, ready to blow up the depot and the houses around it. Lighting her path with the candle, Kovaleva picked her way among the posts on hands and knees, trying not to touch an uninsulated cable somewhere, and looked for the bomb. And there at the end of the cellar, between posts, she saw a high-explosive bomb lying on its side. Certainly, under such circumstances, it needed unusual will power to act with a clear head.

When she got to the bomb, Kovaleva began to knock the clamp ring off with a hammer. Having removed it with difficulty, she took out the detonator and unscrewed the priming cap. The monster was now harmless. When Kovaleva came out of the cellar, she was asked how she had felt. "I was a little upset," said Anna, "because I was afraid the candle would burn down before I got the detonator unscrewed, but everything turned out all right."

A large crowd behind the cordon looked curiously at Anna with eyes of amazement and love for the fearless, delicate girl who had hurried to meet the deadly threat. Kovaleva disarmed more than forty bombs during the blockade. Fate, if we may use the word, was kind to her, for she remained alive and unharmed. At the present time Anna is an engineer in Leningrad.

By their devotion to duty but at the cost of many lives, the members of the civil defense detachments ended the danger that the city might be demolished by delayed-action bombs. Their fearlessness and tenacity kept the Leningraders' spirit high, that spirit which helped them endure the shocks and terrors of a strange life.

The enemy sent scouts and spies into the city, equipped with portable radio transmitters and rockets in order to direct the fire of their artillery and lead their bombers to the most important targets. They were quickly hunted down; people actively assisted the authorities in waging a successful struggle with enemy agents.

Fascist propagandists tried in various ways to exert an ideological influence on the Russian population in the occupied territory but gave most of their attention to units of the Soviet army. In order to make their propaganda believable, the radio broadcasts would call the attention of the listener to the facts of some Soviet military operation that had been unsuccessful and then would vent poisonous slander on Soviet military leaders, blaming them for the retreats and the casualties. Goebbels' entire arsenal of propaganda weapons was used to undermine the authority of the commanders of the Soviet army. To exploit our difficulties in supplying the people with food, enemy aircraft dropped inflammatory leaflets, urging citizens not to obey the authorities. All day and night their radio transmitters broadcast "news" in Russian. They played records over the radio and then declared that soloists of the Academic State Theater were actually at the microphone, using the names of popular Soviet artists. They put out a newspaper in Russian called "Pravda," whose format and type resembled that *Pravda* familiar to the whole Soviet people; in short, they tried to pass this forgery off for the real newspaper. Articles in their paper were falsely signed with the names of persons prominent in the arts, science, and the government. The inventive Nazis tried many other tricks, though they did not succeed. Propaganda founded on falsity can never flourish.

September was unusually warm. In the gardens and parks the grass was still green. The leaves on the trees were blazing with the bright colors of early autumn. Instead of the usual shroud of damp fog hanging over the city, the friendly sun shone, shedding light upon the earth. People did not notice the marvelous days of the golden season however; their thoughts and feelings were in crying contradiction to the nature around them. Instead of happiness and peace, they were filled with anger and hatred of the enemy who had ringed the giant city in an iron hoop. Unprecedented in its severity, a struggle for existence had begun.

Control of military operations and the economic activity of the city's enterprises was exercised from Smolny. Every day enemy aircraft tried to find this well-known building but never located it. It was carefully camouflaged; the central entrance, columns, and stairway were concealed under a thick camouflage netting. The roof and the walls facing the Neva were painted to match the autumn leaves of the surrounding park. From the air the building blended with the treetops. The Germans bombed the square at random, using the Okhtensky Bridge as reference point. The people at Smolny ran great risks, but the work of this large headquarters was not interrupted for a minute day or night. The command post was here too, but underground. In a sealed-off room, teletype machines were set up on long tables; behind each machine sat a female operator wearing military uniform. Absorbed in their work, the girls would tap out the dry telegraphic staccato. Here reports, summaries, and inquiries were received from all sides and sectors of the front. From here headquarters' orders and directives were sent out. It was close in the room; there was not enough oxygen.

The German occupation of the left bank of the Neva from Schluesselburg to the mouth of the Tosno River created a real threat to Leningrad. The enemy could cross the river, since there were no fortified positions on the right bank. With the onset of freezing weather and the formation of ice on the river, the menace of such a crossing increased. The headquarters of the Leningrad Front created the "Neva Fortified Position" to prevent any surprise. Its mission was to protect communication by water along the river, destroy enemy attempts at a crossing, and give artillery support to those troops of the Front operating within range of the Neva Fortified Position's artillery. The Baltic Fleet supplied the NFP with its personnel and guns.

The loss of Schluesselburg at once caused serious difficulties in the city. Ammunition of types and sizes that Leningrad did not produce itself, provisions, fuel, medicines, and much else that was vitally necessary for life and defense, ceased to be delivered to the city. And the enemy was pressing hard. Violent fighting was in progress. Large numbers of casualties were arriving from the battlefield. It was just then that evacuation of the wounded had to be stopped. In response, the Military Council ordered the number of hospitals in the city increased. University buildings, the Herzen Institute, the Palace of Labor, the Technological Institute, the Evropaiskaya and Angleterre hotels, and many others were commandeered for hospitals. By the same order, each chairman of the executive committee of a *raion* soviet became responsible for finding beds, mattresses, pillows, utensils, and kitchenware in his *raion*. In six days a supplementary hospital system was opened with 19,000 beds. Conditions for treating the wounded were made quite satisfactory, which contributed to a speedy convalescence and return to duty—a most important factor, since outside reinforcements were not available at this time.

By command of Voroshilov, the soldiers and officers who were discharged from the hospitals were usually sent back to their old units. This was what they wanted themselves. Their friends gladly welcomed their return, for comradeship in arms is firm and lasting. The veterans soon got back into the rhythm of front-line existence; they were the basic framework on which unit commanders depended.

On September 9 the Military Council decided to construct a port on the small bay of Osinovets on the western shore of Lake Ladoga, nineteen kilometers from Schluesselburg, to receive cargoes and send certain types of rare equipment out of the city. The man whom the Military Council made responsible for building and organizing the port at Osinovets was the second-in-command of the Ladoga naval flotilla, Captain Avraamov. Time limits were set for putting the harbor into operation: first stage (handling five barges a day) by September 18, and second stage (handling twelve vessels a day) by September 25.

The task of defending the new harbor against attack from the lake was assigned to the Ladoga naval flotilla; anti-aircraft units were assigned to protect it from air attacks. The Neva Fortified Position, which was still in process of creation, protected Osinovets against attack from the direction of the Neva. The dual task

31

of building the port and handling ships proved to be beyond the powers of the fussy and indecisive Avraamov. To build a port rapidly, beat off incessant enemy air attacks, unload and load vessels in record time, and assure their safety while under way demanded a leader with strong will, iron nerves, and outstanding organizing ability. On September 19, after considering the situation with respect to deliveries of cargo, the Military Council decided to put Admiral I. S. Isakov (now fleet admiral of the Soviet Union), a member of the Military Council, in charge of transport. Isakov attacked the difficult problem with relish. Like a plowman carving a furrow in unplowed land, he deepened the stony bottom of the inhospitable lake and built jetties along its desolate shore. Day after day he went around the area five to seven times, cheering up and inspiring tired laborers, soldiers, and sailors. Isakov did succeed in accomplishing a great deal, most of all in increasing deliveries of cargoes, but he was not destined to bring what he had begun to completion. German activities in the Baltic Sea required his return to naval duties. Construction of the port at Osinovets was finished long after the prescribed dates.[2]

From the very first days of the siege, Leningrad experienced a shortage of electric power because of lack of fuel. From September on, the use of electricity was drastically curtailed in all enterprises and installations and for the daily needs of the population. Kronstadt switched over to using power from its own "block station."[3] Two coal-heated boilers that had been dismantled as unnecessary in peacetime were put in working order. At Hydroelectric Station No. 5, an oil-burning boiler was converted to burn milled peat. With the help of city workers, the peat plants on the right bank of the Neva delivered 225 carloads of peat every twenty-four hours. Coal stored at Avtovo Station was transported to the power plants by the efforts of the railway men.

These measures, however, and many others undertaken by the Military Council and the party and Soviet organizations in the

[2] The construction of the port is discussed in more detail in chapter vi, "Transportation of Supplies by Water and Air."

[3] A power plant with a limited area of operation within which electric power is strictly regulated.

city proved to be inadequate because there was still too little coal and peat within the ring of the blockade. It was necessary to decrease consumption of electric power continually, worsening living conditions and making production of necessary defense material much more difficult.

To assure a reserve of electric power under any conditions for some of the most important plants, the Military Council decided to make use of two ships with powerful turbo-electric generators. The ships were provided with a full supply of fuel and moored at appropriate spots in the Neva. Other ships were prepared as well, and mobile transformer installations, and specialists were trained to restore the electric power supply as quickly as possible in case the flow of current was interrupted.

After the first violent air raid the Military Council and the civilian authorities became very concerned about the protection of the water supply and the sewage system. A city of two-and-one-half million inhabitants is in mortal danger without water and without sewage disposal. On September 13 the Military Council decided to give protection to the water system as a military objective of exceptional importance. Brigades of specialists in repairing and restoring water mains were formed to do regular tours of duty; they were drawn from workers exempt from military service, engineers, technicians, office workers, those working in the plants and on the water mains and sewer lines. The Fascists did not succeed in putting the city's water system out of commission by bombing and artillery fire, but they caused severe damage every day to its ramified subterranean economy. Freezing weather, however, proved to be more dangerous to the population than bombs; in January the water mains froze. What had been feared most of all happened. Water began to be carried in buckets from the Neva, Fontanka, Moika, and Karpovka.[4]

Enemy aircraft attacked several times each day in September. In every case an alert would be sounded, regardless of the number of airplanes. People went down to the shelters—cellars or specially dug slit trenches—and stayed there, sometimes as long as six

[4] The Neva, only fifty miles long but wide, flows from Lake Ladoga to the Gulf of Finland. The other waterways are tributaries. See Map 3.—Ed.

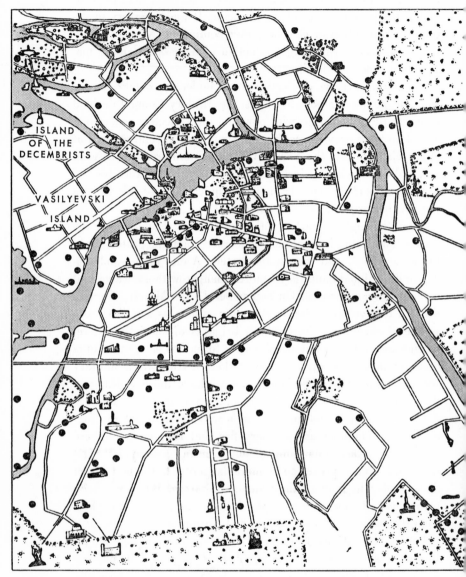

MAP 3.—The city of Leningrad. The black dots indicate places subjected to the heaviest artillery fire and air bombardment.

hours until the "all-clear" was sounded. This mass diversion of several hundred thousand factory and office workers from their duties caused substantial losses. It was thus decided that if only one or two aircraft appeared, the alert would not be sounded. The workers then insisted that work should not be stopped even though a larger number of bombers came over if there was no direct threat to a particular factory. This patriotic request was granted, but the anti-aircraft defenses were now obliged to be extremely vigilant. Our aircraft were constantly on patrol over the city, and when danger was sighted, thousands of people took their stand on the roofs of houses, scanning the sky.

As soon as an artillery bombardment began, the population was notified by radio, by which means people were told what streets and squares were under fire; pedestrians were told which side of the street to walk on; traffic in the danger zone was halted. At first the bombardments made the inhabitants nervous. Often people were killed before one's eyes by shell bursts, or buildings were demolished. But there was no panic. Public institutions functioned as usual. For the convenience of the population, the stores were kept open from 6:00 A.M. to 9:00 P.M. Factory and office workers arrived at work on time, overcoming numerous obstacles on the way.

The enemy bombarded the city at various times of day, but he would open heavy fire when the workday was beginning or had just ended and the streets were full of people, obviously try-ing to hit as many people as possible. Such tactics on the part of the Fascists, aimed at mass slaughter of peaceful inhabitants, were monstrous and senseless and can only be explained as stupid revenge, the result of helpless fury at the besieged.

The Military Council did everything possible to protect the citizenry from this Fascist banditry. Our aircraft constantly kept under observation the area believed to be the site of the enemy's heavy batteries. Our gunners took bearings on the location of the enemy guns by their first shots and began counter-battery fire at different ranges, after which the bombardment of the city would stop; it was later learned that numbers of German artillery men were killed and many guns destroyed by the accurate fire of the defenders. In fear of our counterfire the Germans resorted to hit-and-run artillery attacks: they would fire a few rounds and then change position. Even under these circumstances the Fascist bandits did not go unpunished.

A remarkable feature of the defense of the city was that the whole population was organized and took an active part in it. It can be said without exaggeration that almost every one of the inhabitants was involved. Every night more than sixty thousand men and women of the "self-defense" groups were watching on the roofs. They helped the civil defense units warn the people of threatening danger and found time to study the various ways of extinguishing incendiary bombs. Not only adults, but young people, too, shortly learned how to deal with incendiaries and they disposed of thousands of them safely. Widespread and timely training in disarming bombs played a very important part in the defense of the city, as is shown by the following facts: on October 13 enemy aircraft dropped more than twelve thousand incendiary bombs on the city, or almost twice as many as on September 8, the day of the biggest raid, and these caused forty fires, less than one-fourth the number on September 8. These fires were quickly brought under control. Vigorous military defense was effectively supplemented by civil defense for which a vast multitude of people volunteered, and it was precisely this that prevented the enemy from severing the vital nerves of the huge city despite frantic efforts by the Luftwaffe. The example of the Leningraders confirms the fact that successful resistance to a formidable enemy depends not only on the armed forces but on the active participation of the people as a whole as well.

The city's ground anti-aircraft defense was commanded by Major General E. S. Lagutkin from the first days of the war to its end. His personal qualities—liveliness, good humor, and alertness in reacting to unexpected events—were very valuable under the tense conditions of constant alarms and violent bombardments. His decisive actions and ability to convince others helped in obtaining quickly all sorts of the most modern equipment for the anti-aircraft defense.

Chief Marshal of Artillery N. N. Voronov devoted much effort to organizing the artillery defenses. He was the representative of Supreme Headquarters in Leningrad during the most difficult period. During the critical days of the siege, his calm, well-thought-out orders inspired confidence in his leadership. His tall figure could often be seen at the batteries of long-range artillery firing on enemy positions, at the command posts of army formations, in the shops of major factories; and everywhere Voronov left the deep imprint of his useful presence.

During the assault on our defense lines and in the period of the siege, our own artillery showed its power, as it emerged victorious in the contest with the artillery of the Fascists. The Baltic Fleet also performed significant service in defense of the city. Kronstadt's forts with their formidable guns and naval artillery laid down heavy fire on enemy positions, causing serious loss of life and equipment. From September, 1941, through January, 1942, the Baltic Fleet fired 71,508 heavy-caliber shells at enemy troops.

The artillery fire of our besieged forces caused terror in the enemy ranks, and German soldiers wrote about it in their letters home. In September, 1941, an unfinished letter to his wife was found on the body of a soldier named Henning which read:

> I got through the last attack all right though it was a little rough on me. The Russian fire was inhuman. Our regiment lost 190 dead, not counting the wounded and missing. The Russians raked over every bit of ground with fire from all types of weapons but we still came out healthy and got our first chance to rest because a reserve unit relieved us during the night. For weeks we did not have time to think of ourselves for we lived like animals, with almost no water till today. We ate once a day, iron rations at that, with very long marches. But now we'll rest a couple of days and everybody is glad he can put his rifle down for once.

From the diary of *Unteroffizier* Kuechnel:

> Thursday, Sept. 18, 1941. Poured rain during the night. Heavy fire from enemy light and heavy artillery lasted a long time. At dawn we were much surprised by rifle fire from the other side. Four killed, several wounded. *Unteroffizier* Schloss, *Unteroffizier* Kluege, Oschz, and Mueller fell.
>
> Sunday, Sept. 21, 1941. I think since Sept. 13 we have lost more than fifty men here. Enemy artillery is giving us a

lot of trouble right now. At noon, the usual time, artillery and mortar fire.

Saturday, Sept. 27, 1941. In a straight line it's eleven to fifteen kilometers to Lake Ladoga and the Neva. I think today was the worst I have gone through. We came under artillery fire after no more than five minutes of marching.

Tuesday, Sept. 30, 1941. The Russians didn't throw hand-grenades yesterday. At twelve o'clock an awful salvo from mortars hit our position . . . the *Gefreiter* was killed, nine fellows were killed by a direct hit. Some were right in front of my shelter. Today at noon they were hitting the front line trenches hard . . . one mortar shell dropped right in, killed five or six men; I think one was one of mine. Two men were sent up as observers, one of them was wounded then and there. This evening ten more men and one officer were killed.

From an unsent letter by a soldier named Guenther to his sister Gerta dated September 21, 1941:

I'm sitting in a trench and want to write you a few lines. The Russian artillery doesn't give us any rest and when it stops some crazy tank starts shooting. I've had a belly full. The weather stays very bad, rain three days in a row. Everything is damp and at night there's hoarfrost and it freezes. We are south of Lake Ladoga.

From the diary of *Unteroffizier* Viktor Kolodsit:

Wednesday, Oct. 1, 1941. Now October has really arrived. Till this morning I didn't believe we would still be here. At 11:00 the enemy artillery got to work. Indescribably heavy artillery fire from all sides. Many killed and wounded.

There were a great many letters of this sort, testifying to the force and effectiveness of the defenders' fire and the low morale of the German "Goliaths."

The enemy tried with all his might to annihilate the artillery of the besieged city and thereby weaken its defense. With no regard for losses, Fascist headquarters threw hundreds of aircraft against Kronstadt, its forts and ship anchorages, but achieved no success. Fire from the anti-aircraft guns was so heavy that the enemy airplanes stayed at a great height and after dropping their bombs at random hurried to get out of range. From July through November, 1941, the city's anti-aircraft guns and fighter aviation downed 555 enemy airplanes; this was a fearful blow to the Luftwaffe and from the end of November on, air attacks on Leningrad were weaker.

A great responsibility rested on the leaders of the defense of Leningrad. On their courage, skill, and insight much depended, first of all the morale of the troops and the population. Voroshilov and Zhdanov kept in constant touch with the inhabitants of the beleaguered city. The people loved them and believed in them as they themselves devoutly believed in victory during the most difficult, desperate, days of fighting. Zhdanov stayed in Leningrad almost to the end of the war. Knowing the locality well, he went up to the front line often to find out personally the true state of affairs and to lend the men moral support. In November, while up with the troops, Zhdanov learned that German front-line units were equipped with skis and white cloaks. When he returned to Leningrad, he sent for the chief of the rear, Major General Lagunov, and demanded an explanation for our front-line units not being supplied with skis and camouflage clothing. Lagunov reported that the clothing would be ready in six or seven days; the delay had occurred because the order arrived late at the factories. As for the skis there had been a slip-up: very few of them were on hand in the supply warehouses. After thinking a moment Lagunov added: "Civilians and civilian organizations have skis and don't need them now, but it will take time to collect them. Supply didn't think it would snow this early and that winter would come so soon."

Lagunov's report upset Zhdanov; he got up and paced the small oblong room several times, then stopped in front of a map on which the front line was drawn in bright color. This ill-omened line surrounded Leningrad like a noose. Zhdanov said: "The Germans have already put their units in the Schluesselburg area on skis although they don't even know how to ski properly. But we are not ready. Carelessness, criminal carelessness! Winter wasn't expected until December, but it came, didn't it, in the first days of November. War creates unexpected problems, Comrade Lagunov," Zhdanov continued angrily, "and we have to know how to solve them fast, but you and Supply were fast asleep. Compatriots like you really grieve me; you are a Russian, you can and you ought to be ahead of these foreigners." He added quietly: "I'm giving you three days. If by the end of that time the skis and white cloaks aren't ready, remember this: we are in a besieged fortress, and siege law is severe on those who violate it."

Zhdanov thought highly of Lagunov for his knowledge, honesty, and honorableness. But where defense was concerned he would not forgive the slightest slip. The general took vigorous actions: day and night the clothing factories and shops of the Producer's Co-operatives sewed camouflage cloaks; skis were collected from every side and sent to the troops. Zhdanov's order was carried out on time.

With the arrival of cold weather, industrial enterprises began to stop work. Transportation virtually halted in the city. The public baths were closed; on rare occasions during the winter of 1941–42 seven or eight baths would be heated. There was not food enough. In most houses the windows had been broken by blast waves and were boarded up with plywood or planks; living quarters were dark and cold. The residential neighborhoods beyond Narvskaya Zastava and in the Moskovsky and Volodarsky *raions,* lying nearest the front line, were subjected to the most frequent and most intense artillery fire. To save human lives the City Soviet and *raion* executive committees moved 54,000 people from these neighborhoods to less dangerous *raions.* It was a very complicated matter to relocate them, however. Living quarters became overcrowded. Lodgers were deprived of the most elementary facilities. After every air raid a certain number of citizens had no roofs over their heads; they had to be moved into already overcrowded living space. It was growing hard to live. Unexpected events turned people's habitual way of life upside down.

Many complicated problems confronted the Leningrad City Executive Committee every day. The chairman of the Executive

Committee, P. S. Popkov, knew the city's economy well, and this helped him solve immediate questions with dispatch. The City Party Committee and the Leningrad Front Military Council backed him fully in his work. Seldom to be found at Smolny during the opening days of the siege, he paid frequent visits to factories, electric power plants, and neighborhoods that had been subjected to air bombardment and assisted the victims as much as he could. His enterprise in practical affairs did much to improve co-operation among the factories and increase production of arms. Particularly large amounts of his time and effort he spent organizing the procurement of firewood and peat to keep the electric power plants, the defense factories, and food enterprises functioning. Popkov was always excited; he worked heartily and hard with a certain ardor, although at times he had to break off because he could not always control his shaky nerves. But these were minor deviations in a many-sided and untiring labor.

With every passing day the Leningraders felt the blows of the war more keenly; the city was being destroyed before their eyes, factories were closing, food was getting worse. Feelings of uneasiness about the future grew. In response to this attitude of mind on the part of the people, the City Party Committee called a meeting of party "activists" in the meeting hall at Smolny where Zhdanov delivered a short speech. He reported on the situation and described the position of the enemy troops as unenviable, though they were entrenched on the outskirts of Leningrad. He said that behind the paling of Fascist guns bombarding the city could be seen the beginning of the collapse of the German army. At the same time he warned that the population had to know about the obvious hardships Leningrad would face. For a certain length of time, these could not be avoided. "The Russians have looked death in the face many times," said Zhdanov, "and displayed strength of spirit as they did it; this time too they will not tremble, but we must tell the people the truth, just as it is, and they will understand us." Speaking of the approaching shortages of food and fuel, he called for the strictest economizing. "The main task of the Communists, the Comsomols, and the whole population is to save what supplies we have, to make them last a long time. We have to win time, to fight with all our might to make more shells, military equipment, guns. Women and young people must replace men in the factories." Zhdanov described the measures being taken by headquarters and the City Party Committee for organizing deliveries of food and other supplies to Leningrad over Lake Ladoga and ended with these words: "The Central Committee of the Communist Party and the Government are watching our front and are taking the necessary steps. The time is not far off, comrades, when the enemy army will certainly be beaten."[5]

The party organization strengthened the people in their struggle to overcome difficulties, explained the situation, and helped the weak to banish the fear that was born of dangers.

In his book, *The Discovery of India,* Jawaharlal Nehru writes: "Fear creates phantoms which are more terrible than reality itself, while reality, if we deal with it calmly and are ready for any trial, becomes considerably less terrifying." And during those first days of the siege, as the enemy exerted all the pressure he could on the collective mind of the population, creating phantoms more terrible than reality itself, the Communists by their energetic actions frustrated the stealth of the enemy; they inculcated confidence in victory and exhorted the people not to wait passively for help from outside but to mobilize all the strength and resources of the beleaguered city. Bravely, the people prepared to meet the hungry winter that was approaching, adapting themselves to a new life of alarms and surprises.

The moral force of the Leningraders was displayed in the most varied aspects of life and had a decisive effect upon the outcome of the siege. The spiritual strength of the population was particularly clearly expressed during the period of the greatest exhaustion of material resources. Although by that time food had become something to dream of, nobody grumbled. People worked at their posts to their last breath. It was just this strength that guided the activities of the people and led to victory.

[5] The words of Zhdanov are quoted from the author's notes.

3

FOOD RESOURCES

September–December, 1941

THE INVASION OF the Soviet Union and the enemy's rapid advance into the interior of the country placed the national economy under great strain. The territories occupied by the Germans in the period through October, 1941, had produced 38 per cent of the prewar gross output of grain, 84 per cent of the sugar, 63 per cent of the coal, 68 per cent of the cast iron, and 60 per cent of the aluminum. They contained 38 per cent of the total number of large horned cattle and 60 per cent of the total number of pigs.[1] The loss of so much productive capacity acutely affected the raw material and general economic potential of the country at the same time that the army had to have supplies of food, fuel, ammunition, and other material speedily. Moreover, many factories in the western parts of the country which had been scheduled in peacetime plans to produce and furnish goods for the national economy were now compelled to relocate in the east. People moved, bag and baggage, in an endless stream. Factories were evacuated with their machines and equipment. Cattle were driven off. It was as though the earth reared up and everything animate and inanimate rolled from west to east. Even amid this chaos of hasty, seemingly incomprehensible displacement, however, the guiding thread of economic direction was not lost.

The durability of a state always depends in large part on

[1] See N. Voznesensky, *The War Economy of the USSR during the Fatherland War* (Moscow: State Political Publishing House, 1948), p. 42.

43

prompt and exact fulfilment by men of their obligations. Under exceptional circumstances, the requirement is absolute. Despite the monstrous difficulties, Soviet men and women did not lose their heads during the war. They continued to do their duty, wherever they happened to be. In this lay the strength of our state, as it still does.

Strict centralization of economic direction made it possible to distribute material resources where they were needed most. The armed forces and civilian population were supplied with many kinds of goods that were distributed immediately on arrival.

The period of greatest difficulty for the country coincided with the developing struggle of the besieged to defend Leningrad.

Having seized the Baltic provinces, enemy forces invaded the Pskov and Novgorod areas at the beginning of July. Governmental authorities and economic organizations hurriedly began to evacuate the more important kinds of equipment from the threatened regions. What there was no time to evacuate was destroyed. Particular haste was made to rescue the grain stored in special granaries, and about three million poods[2] were brought through safely in the very face of the enemy's forward units, thanks to the coolness and decisive action of granary and railroad workers.

Amid the turmoil of those days, mistakes were made in the routing of trains. Instead of dispatching the trains of evacuated goods and raw materials to Leningrad, where they could have been unloaded quickly, freeing the cars for other freight while the goods and raw materials were used for the city's needs, numbers of trains were sent east. At the same time, through freight trains carrying the same kinds of goods and raw materials were hurrying from the central provinces to Leningrad. Just when the railroads were most overloaded, paradoxical as it seems, such trains were passing each other, to the detriment of the effort to evacuate the most important types of equipment and other goods. This and other similar examples show how the path of concrete action was studded with difficulties at the beginning of the war.

[2] A pood is equivalent to 36.113 lbs. "Special granaries" contained emergency stores of grain. The system had been developed by Stalin in the period of collectivization.—Ed.

These difficulties were often enough the result of the multiplicity of administrative authorities and the lack of co-ordination among their plans. The mistakes nevertheless cannot cast into shadow the services of workers, railroad men, and state employees, who under the enemy's fire were able to rescue everything that might have strengthened him.

As the fighting drew nearer and approached the immediate vicinity of Leningrad, it became very difficult to supply the population and the troops with food. Expenditures of food from the city's reserves rose sharply. Beginning early in September the through freights which had made daily deliveries of provisions from the central regions of the country to the supply services of the army and the Baltic Fleet ceased to arrive. From then on, the troops and the sailors of the Baltic Fleet had to be fed from the city's supplies. In addition, Leningrad was now crowded with more than one hundred thousand refugees from the Baltic republics: from Pskov, Luga, Petrozavodsk, from the Karelian Isthmus, and from workers' settlements. Abandoning their homes, the people had fled toward the interior of the country but managed no farther than Leningrad because railroads and other roads had been cut. The refugees lived in freight cars shunted onto sidings in Leningrad, suffering discomforts and privations. They waited patiently, hoping the enemy would soon be driven off the roads he had severed and that the crowded freight cars would move on. Their hopes were vain. When cold weather came, the refugees were removed to barracks and given shelter. Whether working or fighting, every adult person was needed in the defense of Leningrad. The limited food supply, however, urgently required that the number of mouths to be fed in the city should be lowered rather than increased by evacuating as many people as possible. But it was already too late. Supplies were being reduced, and food consumption was increasing. The slowness about evacuating the population during July and August can be explained largely by the fact that the inhabitants did not sense a direct threat and therefore did not wish to leave. Leningrad's civilian authorities, too, hardly believed that the Germans would actually reach Leningrad *oblast*. A typical episode demonstrates their incredulity.

Children began to be evacuated at the end of June and the beginning of July. But where should they be sent? While a few trainloads of children were sent off to Yaroslavsk *oblast*,[3] most of the children were sent to places in Leningrad *oblast*, around Luga, Tolmachevo, Gatchina, and other normal peacetime vacation spots for children: in other words, into the path of the advancing enemy. The danger of the situation was not really grasped until enemy tanks were already speeding toward Luga with Pskov behind them. The children who had been dispatched so fast toward the front were now retrieved. After some time, several tens of thousands were again evacuated deep within the zone of the interior. They would be separated from their parents, who would endure incredible difficulties during the period, for about three years.

It was hard for mothers to part from children being evacuated to far-distant regions (Kirovsk, Sverdlovsk *oblasts*).[4] Tears were shed at parting and more grief remained in parents' hearts unwept. Before long, however, alarm for the fate of the children turned into a sense of relief, for the children were safe. The authorities had created the conditions necessary for their training and education, and they were housed in comfortable, warm quarters, supplied with good food, and surrounded by care and attention. The children who stayed in Leningrad for various reasons, on the other hand, suffered grave privation despite the concern of their own parents and of the city and *raion* authorities and the public in general. Their pure eyes saw too much sorrow and suffering. Nights made fearful by bombardment, the horror of homes being destroyed, the deaths of those near and dear could not leave the impressionable souls of young children untouched. One can only strongly regret what occurred.

The rate of evacuation was held back by the conviction, shared by the population and the municipal party and Soviet organizations, that the enemy would not get close to Leningrad. In large

[3] Yaroslavsk *oblast* is located northeast of Moscow.—Ed.

[4] Kirovsk *oblast* is slightly north and east of Gorky. Sverdlovsk *oblast* is in the Ural region, east of Moscow.—Ed.

part, those who went were the families of workers whose factories had previously been moved to the eastern sections of the country. No more than 400,000 people[5] were evacuated to the interior over great reluctance during July and August, whereas the number should have been two or three times higher. Some representatives of local authorities viewed the refusal of citizens to be evacuated as a patriotic action and were proud of it, thus involuntarily encouraging people to remain.

Often it was said: "Our people are ready to work in the front lines but not to leave Leningrad." The argument reflected the mood of the Leningraders but could not be accepted. Old people, invalids, and children did not work, yet their presence in the city meant expenditure of already scanty supplies of food besides the constant worry on the part of parents for the safety of their children. Another factor in the reluctance must also be taken into account here. During July and the first half of August most Leningraders did not know exactly where the German forces were. They did not know what fortified lines stood between them and the enemy. The city was not subjected to bombardment during the period, which contributed to the general mood of calm. Needed were drastic administrative measures to require people to leave the city, as the course of events demanded. Such meas-

[5] According to official sources, 636,283 people were evacuated from Leningrad during the period from June 29 through August 27, 1941 (Leningrad Party Archive: Record Group 24, Inventory No. 26, File Unit 6237, p. 45), but the refugees from the Baltic republics, the Karelo–Finnish SSR, the Leningrad and Pskov *oblasts*, are included in this figure and this is not directly relevant to my subject. We are not discussing the total number of people evacuated over the Leningrad railroad network, but only the total number of Leningraders who were evacuated. It is this aspect which is of interest in the analysis and description of subsequent events. It must be noted, furthermore, that for various reasons a number of those evacuated in June and July returned to Leningrad in August, but no list of these people, of course, was ever made.

If we start with the total population of Leningrad as of January 1, 1941, subtract the (estimated) number of those called up for army service and the total of the remaining population (computed on the basis of numbers of ration cards issued in September plus the number of those who ate at a mess), then the total number of Leningraders that were evacuated turns out to have been no more than 400,000.

ures, however, were resorted to only with caution. The result was that a civilian population of 2,544,000, including about 400,000 children, was left in the blockaded city. Another 343,000 people stayed in suburban areas within the ring of blockade.[6] With the beginning of systematic bombings, artillery bombardments, and fires in September, thousands of families would have liked to leave, but the roads had been cut. A mass evacuation of civilians began only in January over the Ice Road.

There is no doubt that the slowness about evacuating people was tolerated in the opening period of the war (June–August). Only extra difficulties resulted from the large numbers of children, women, old people, and invalids who thus remained in the beleaguered city.

On the evening of September 6, an alarming code telegram from Popkov, the chairman of the Leningrad City Executive Committee, was received at the State Defense Committee. He reported that only very little food was left in the city and requested that the dispatch of food trains be expedited. But what could be done? The enemy was already encircling the city. Despite the bravery of the railroad workers, trains could not be moved through. On September 8 Leningrad was gripped in fearsome pincers by the Fascist armies.

General headquarters and Leningrad Front headquarters were very much affected by this development. They took strenuous measures to break through the enemy lines from the direction of Mga. The Leningraders lived in hopes of such a breakthrough. Until the blockade should be breached there was only one way out: to economize food by every means while preparing a water route for supplying food by way of Lake Ladoga as quickly as possible.

On September 8 the State Defense Committee (SDC) dispatched its own representative to Leningrad. He had full powers to deal with problems of food supplies for the troops of the Front

[6] The figures for Leningrad were obtained from records of the ration cards issued in September and the number of those eating at a mess (estimated); for the suburbs, from a report of the *oblast* executive committee on September 20, 1941.

and the population of the city. On September 10 and 11 he made a detailed inventory of all food supplies at the disposal of civilian and military authorities. The inventory showed slightly more food on hand than Popkov had reported to the SDC. On the basis of the actual rate of expenditure in supplying troops and population, remaining supplies on September 12 were as given in Table 1.

TABLE 1

	Supply (In Days)
Bread grain, flour, and zwieback	35
Cereals* and macaroni (including flour intended for making macaroni)	30
Meat and meat products (including live cattle for slaughter)	33
Fats	45
Sugar and confectionery	60

* Buckwheat, millet, rice, semolina, etc.—Ed.

Canned goods and hardtack kept by the ground forces and fleet as emergency rations are not included in these figures, nor is a small quantity of flour which was stored on special ships of the Baltic Fleet for emergencies. In any case, however, the total amount of supplies was extremely small and gave cause for serious alarm.[7] There was no use hoping, however, that food would arrive

[7] In some books and articles the amount of food available as of September 6, 1941, is given as less than my figures in this book, the authors citing as source the estimate of the Leningrad City Party Committee (Leningrad Party Archive: Record Group 25, Inventory No. 15, File Unit 143, pp. 75–78). In this estimate it is stated: "From September on, when the city of Leningrad was blockaded by the enemy and railroad connections with the rest of the country were severed, the city's food resources, as of September 6, were capable of supplying the population as follows: flour, 14.1 days; cereals, 23 days; meat and meat products, 18.7 days; fats, 20.8 days; sugar and confectionery, 47.9 days."
The first thing to be noted about these figures is that the estimate refers only to supplying the civilian population with the remaining food resources without including the needs of the troops and the amount of provisions under the control of the supply services of the Front and the Baltic Fleet. This fact alone would prevent readers from obtaining a true picture of the food supplies still available to the besieged. Actually, from the first day of the blockade on, the troops of the Front, the crews of the Baltic Fleet, and the civilian population were fed from the total of supplies available within the ring of blockade, regardless of whether the supplies came

from outside in the near future. The only remaining line of communication with the rest of the country—across Lake Ladoga—was not then equipped either with harbor facilities or approach routes. The number of barges and tugs, moreover, was inadequate. It would require time to put the water road in shape to handle large-scale transport. Meanwhile, the artillery bombardment and fires caused by it were a constant threat to diminish further the inadequate supplies of food. Decisive action was needed quickly, both to preserve and economize the remaining provisions and to discover new sources of nourishment. Under

originally from city, central, or military resources; and it is just this point that is worth knowing.

Moreover, the actual amounts on hand are by no means fully reflected in the above estimate. Thus, for example, it mentions the amount of flour (enough for 14.1 days), but says nothing about the amount of grain on hand, whereas on September 12, besides flour, there were more than 10,000 tons of bread grain, 3,000 tons of hardtack (not counting emergency rations for the troops), and 4,800 tons of soy beans. Inaccuracies in the amount of meat are also present. According to the estimate there was enough meat and meat products for 18.7 days. This figure approximately corresponds to the amount of meat on hand in the refrigerators of the main administration of the meat industry. But this was by no means all the meat available. As of September 12, there were 18,769 pigs in the subsidiaries of the food-producing enterprises, and 4,410 more in the state farms of the Pig Trust. Besides this, there were 4,357 head of large horned cattle in various economic organizations. All this livestock was later slaughtered and the meat put on inventory and into the "general pot" for distribution. There were also seven hundred tons of dressed poultry and a considerable quantity of canned goods. The amounts on hand of fats, sugar, and candy are understated in the estimate.

It is necessary also to note that the daily expenditure of provisions for the civilian population as given in the estimate for September 6 is calculated on a larger scale than was the case in the estimate of September 12, which is explained by the fact that the rations for certain foods, bread in particular, were lower then they had been on the sixth. In calculating how many days the food would last as of September 12, we proceeded from the following data: (a) amount of all kinds of food on hand in the armed forces, the state reserve, and civilian organizations; (b) actual numerical strength of the army and Baltic Fleet and the total number of inhabitants (based on the number of ration cards issued in September) plus the total of those in various detachments and organizations who received their food at a mess; (c) ration quotas for troops and population in effect on that date (for actual amounts of rations, see pp. 86, 88, of this book).

B Kyk

the pressure of the threat of imminent German penetration, however, solution of these problems was temporarily deferred.

The methods then current for storing, preserving, and keeping account of foodstuffs—those concerned with the amount of food distributed especially—were not up to the situation. Grain, flour, and sugar, for example, had been concentrated in two or three places, a piece of shortsighted negligence that would have to be paid for in part. Administrative jurisdiction over food supplies resided in ten different economic agencies. In the absence of instructions from their central offices in Moscow, each of them continued to issue food according to the usual procedures, although conditions in Leningrad were not usual, but extraordinary, by then. The network of commercial dining rooms and restaurants, where food was sold completely without ration cards, continued to operate. Sales through this network were of considerable importance, making up, for example, 12 per cent of the total sales of fats, up to 10 per cent of meat products, and 8 per cent of sugar and confectionery.

The weight of cattle to be slaughtered was estimated only visually. Such an uncertain method could lead to serious miscalculations and to the squandering of meat by the workers in the scattered plants.

Vegetable fats were stored in trade warehouses, animal fats in military supply warehouses, and they were expended unequally and unjustly since there was no single plan of issue.

Only because people did not wish to accept it as part of the fish or meat allotment, canned crabmeat was sold without ration cards. This could hardly be justified as a policy after September 8 when there had ceased to be any possibility of customers exercising choice among foods. The existence of the population's food supply was in fact under threat from that date. The highly nourishing goods were nonetheless sold without restriction and without being marked off on the ration card.

Invalids and children were supplied with food in hospitals and children's homes, besides holding ration cards through which additional food could be obtained.

The war in Leningrad had become a struggle of the sharpest

kind from the day the siege began. The arena of military operations was streets, squares, factories, and homes, and the entire
population—including the young, the elderly, and the sick—was
affected. Victory now depended on time, for which it was necessary to hold out. For this reason no exceptions could be made.
Every ton of food had to be valued as a part of the defense of
the city.

On September 2 the Leningrad City Executive Committee approved the first reduction of sales of bread to the civilian population since the issue of ration cards. From that day on, factory
workers were issued 600 grams of bread a day, office workers 400
grams, dependents and children 300 grams.[8] Even after the reduction of the bread ration the consumption of flour remained
high: more than two thousand tons a day. Many foodstuffs were
still being sold unrationed. The State Defense Committee demanded categorically that the Military Council take drastic measures to economize on the expenditure of food supplies.

Following the directive of the SDC, the Military Council took
a number of further steps toward economizing food in conjunc-
tion with the City Party Committee and the Leningrad City Executive Committee. Their decisions were primarily directed toward
the most efficient use of raw materials and food products and their
careful storage; the discovery of additional sources of nourishment; and the keeping of accurate records and control over all
resources.

The network of public restaurants and dining rooms was eliminated. Production of beer, ice cream, meat pies, and pastry was
discontinued. In the remaining cafeterias and dining rooms (attached to various institutions) part of a meal now counted on a
person's ration card.

Food supplies in the possession of civilian agencies, the army,
and the fleet were strictly itemized. The directors of industrial
enterprises and the supply service of the army had to submit
reports every ten days to the Leningrad City Executive Committee (with copies to the representative of the SDC) on the amounts
of food in their keeping.

[8] A gram equals 0.3527 ounces. Six hundred grams equal about one
pound five ounces.—Ed.

Orders emanating from administrative centers in Moscow concerning expenditures of food were canceled. These belated directives only caused confusion, issued as they were in ignorance of the real situation in Leningrad. The following minor incident is typical of the times. In mid-September, 1941, the central administration of the sugar industry, located in Moscow, wired its Leningrad office to dispatch a number of freight-car loads of sugar from Leningrad to Vologda. Leningrad had been blockaded since September 8. There were many similar cases. Individuals whose duties were connected in some way or other with the front acted on outdated information.

Expenditure of food above the prescribed limits without special permission from the Military Council was strictly forbidden. Livestock that belonged to state or public organizations was ordered to slaughter; the meat was to be sent to city warehouses for distribution, and the fodder grain intended for the animals was used as admixtures in flour.

Hospital patients were required to surrender their ration cards to the hospital administration, which obtained the person's ration as long as he was in the hospital. The same system extended to children in children's homes. It was possible by this strict regime to reduce the number of people receiving double rations by eighty thousand in a month. All these measures, however, were themselves insufficient, for expenditure was still out of proportion to the amount of provisions.

The bread ration was reduced for the second time on September 12. Factory workers were now issued 500 grams of bread, office workers and children 300, dependents 250; personnel who ate at messes (these were mainly students at the industrial and technical schools, fire brigades, militarized security guards of factories and plants, and railroad-transport and civil defense workers) also received 500 grams. Those mobilized for building fortifications received 500 grams per day. The executive committees of the *raion* soviets and the managers of plants and enterprises were instructed in this case to confiscate the ration cards of those called up to work for the city in order to avoid a double issue of bread while they were thus employed.

New and reduced rations were also established for meat and cereals.[9] They are listed in grams per month in Table 2.

For sugar and confectionery and fats the quotas were somewhat higher than those in force in a number of other cities in the Soviet Union, owing to the need to make up at least in part for the lower rations of meat, cereals, and vegetables. The inhabitants

TABLE 2

	Meat	Cereals
Workers.................	1,500*	1,500
Office Workers............	800	1,000
Dependents..............	400	600
Children under 12.........	400	1,200

* Workers thus received approximately 3 lb. 5 oz. of meat per month and the same amount of cereals.

TABLE 3

	Sugar and Confectionery	Fats
Workers.................	2,000	950
Office Workers............	1,700	500
Dependents..............	1,500	300
Children under 12.........	1,700	500

TABLE 4

	Sugar and Confectionery	Fats
Workers.................	1,500	600
Office Workers............	1,000	250
Dependents..............	800	200
Children under 12.........	1,200	500

of Leningrad received the amounts (in grams per month) listed in Table 3.

The amount of sugar and fats on hand, however, did not permit this ration to be maintained for long. In November new quotas were established, which are listed in Table 4 in grams per month.

[9] Initial ration quotas and their subsequent alterations are shown on p. 88.

Looking back from the vantage point of today when it is easy to calculate down to the single gram, it may be said that the fats ration, most clearly, and the sugar ration should not have been increased in September. The approximately 2,500 tons of sugar and 600 tons of fats expended in September and October to provide a supplementary increase in diet would have been extremely valuable in December. During that month of starvation, the issue of bread was completely insufficient, fats were virtually not available to the adult population and were not replaced with substitutes, and other foodstuffs were issued in the most trifling quantities. At the time, however, in September, 1941, the veil of uncertainty obscured much that is clear today. The besieged simply did not imagine that the blockade of the city would last so long.

Salt and matches were sold without restrictions during the first months of the siege. In December, as a measure of precaution, a ration of four hundred grams of salt and four boxes of matches per person, which was completely satisfactory, was established. The population felt no lack of these items in the initial period of the blockade. On the other hand, the inhabitants were in acute need of kerosene. The constant search for kerosene for lighting and cooking the scant food available took a toll in suffering and health. In September 2.5 liters of kerosene per person were issued. With that the issue of kerosene stopped. Kerosene was not again available to the civilian population until February, 1942; only public buildings, hospitals, and children's institutions were lighted. Soap was distributed regularly at two hundred grams per person per month.

The privations that fell thus unexpectedly on the heads of peaceful people did not stop their strenuous activity. The danger forced them to be vigilant and to focus their minds on current problems.

In a concentration that was unjustified and dangerous, almost all the supplies of flour for the population were kept at two milling combines, the Lenin and Kirov. To avoid possible destruction by fire the flour was removed to various warehouses in safer places. Grain was removed from the harbor elevators and warehouses, which were located close to the enemy front line, for the same reason.

Except for the loss from fire of a small quantity of flour and sugar at the Badaev warehouses, the Fascists failed to inflict serious damage on food supplies during the whole period of the blockade. The Badaev loss occurred on September 8, the day of mass air attacks on the city. The old wooden warehouses, built as far back as 1914 by the St. Petersburg merchant Rasteryaev, were ignited quickly by the flames of the incendiary bombs. As the fire gaps between the structures were narrow (ten meters), the flames of one burning warehouse merged with those of the next to form one vast blaze, making it much harder to fight. A great effort on the part of special detachments and workers was required finally to check the fire. In the warehouses were some food supplies for current needs, records, and spare parts and other property belonging to trade organizations. Several days after the fire it was determined that three thousand tons of flour had been destroyed, and about 2,500 tons of lump sugar had been turned into thick syrup with a black crust on top. Later this was made over into confectionery so that the loss of sugar totaled no more than seven hundred tons, according to estimates of workers in the trade.

A detailed description of the fire and the amount of loss is given here only in order to counteract the inventions of writers who tell fables about it. The fire at the Badaev warehouses received considerable attention in our literature in the first years after the war. It was always described, however, in such a way that the reader must conclude that the subsequent hunger in Leningrad resulted from the enormous amount of food that had been destroyed at the warehouses. Since for a while it was nowhere reliably stated how much food had actually been destroyed, the fantasy might be excused. It is another matter now, when the consequences of the fire are widely known. As late as 1960, despite the well-known facts, more fiction was published about vast losses of food. In a pamphlet by T. A. Zhdanova, *Fortress on the Neva*, it is stated:

Enemy high-explosive and incendiary bombs brought dev-astation and destruction to Leningrad's food warehouses. The glow of fires shone above the city. The Badaev warehouses were burning with enough food supplies to last the entire population of Leningrad at least three years and more. Soon the lack of food and fuel would be felt acutely in the besieged city.[10]

Such assertions are based on rumors and conjectures. Permit-ting herself to write that warehouses burned with provisions enough "to last . . . at least three years and more," the author ob-viously has not the slightest idea of the requirements of the popu-lation of Leningrad and hence of the amounts of food involved. She knows even less of the specific matter she is writing about, the Badaev warehouses, their capacity, and what was stored there, let alone the fire itself and its results. Such a carefree attitude to-ward facts that are of real importance in evaluating the situation in the besieged city is intolerable, all the more since the pamphlet was published with the avowed purpose of recreating the spectacle of the historic battle of Soviet people for Lenin's city.

The inhabitants of suburban *raions*—Vsevolzhky, Pargolov-sky, parts of Slutsky, and Oranienbaumsky—were required by a decision of the Military Council to deliver to the state all their potatoes beyond the established ration for personal consumption. For collective farmers raising potatoes on private garden plots, the ration was set at fifteen kilograms per person per month. All potatoes consigned to a seed fund were liable to confiscation by the state. People who concealed vegetables and did not put them on record were brought to account in accordance with wartime laws.

By September 20, 2,352 tons of potatoes and vegetables had been collected at the warehouses of the trade organizations. A great part of the potato crop was still in the ground at the time, however, for the potato fields were exposed to artillery fire. The Germans would open fire on anything moving, and many brave spirits perished. But little time remained to gather the potatoes;

[10] T. A. Zhdanova, *Fortress on the Neva* (Moscow: State Political Pub-lishing House, 1960), p. 28.

winter was at the door. To the help of the collective farmers came workers and office employees from Leningrad. They gathered the potatoes mostly at night, creeping over the fields on hands and knees, hiding in shell holes, lying prone to dig the potatoes up and pile them in heaps. Dry weather favored the gathering-in. Except for a small area where the fields came quite close to the enemy front line, the harvest was gathered and transported. The population received another 7,300 tons of potatoes and vegetables; in all 9,652 tons were collected for distribution, or something less than four kilograms per person. Under these conditions vegetables had to be economized. They were issued very sparingly to military and civilian hospitals, factory cafeterias, and front-line troops. Once in a while a small quantity was sold to the population for a ration coupon good only on that one occasion.

Of all foodstuffs bread bulked the largest in volume. To deliver flour or grain across Lake Ladoga from the "mainland," as the rest of the country outside the ring of defenses was called, in sufficient quantity to supply minimum needs was impossible during the first months of the siege. The problem of bread supply was a matter of life and death. The search began for substitutes which might lessen to some extent the expenditure of bread grains and make them last longer. As the manufacture of beer had been halted, all the malt on hand at the breweries, to the amount of eight thousand tons, was moved to the flour mills, ground, and used as an admixture to bread. The military supply warehouses contained about five thousand tons of oats for feeding horses. The animals had to be deprived of the good feed, sad though it was, and the oats were remilled and used to make bread.

From September 15 on, in view of the amount of grain on hand, bread was prepared with the following composition: rye flour 52 per cent, oats 30 per cent, barley 8 per cent, soy bean 5 per cent, malt 5 per cent.

The supply service faced the problem of feeding the horses once the oats were removed. Horses were economically necessary, but there was nothing to feed them. It was utterly impossible to bring in hay from the mainland. After prolonged search a way out was discovered which hardly pleased the horses, to be sure, but did ease the acute problem of feeding them for a while. The administrations of the Leningrad forest conservation zone and of the October Railroad were charged with procurement of branches (young sprouts); these were cut, bundled, and carted out of the woods. The branches were well stewed in hot water, sprinkled with cotton-seed oil cake, and salt added before feeding them to the horses. Production of a mixed feed using peat was gotten under way at the Lakhtinsky peat factory at the same time. The mixture comprised cotton-seed oil cake, peat shavings, dust from the flour mills, bran, bone meal, and salt. The feed was produced in compressed form in bales weighing up to eighty kilograms. The horses did not like the mixed feed; they preferred the feed made of branches.

The strain of supplying the city with bread required considerable maneuvering with the scanty resources of flour, grain, and admixtures. Thus, to prevent the bread from some factories having a lower percentage of flour substitutes than that of others, the flour admixtures were transported on a daily basis from warehouses and milling combines. In view of the size of the ration, a difference in quality would have provoked justified indignation. The admixtures themselves were prepared from ingredients brought to the mills from ten different places in the city. The shortage of gasoline, the frequent air alerts, artillery fire, blackout conditions, and lack of loading personnel further strained the overworked transport facilities. For round-the-clock operational direction of all transport and loading a dispatcher group of managers was formed at the city office of the State Grain Purchasing Administration.

From the end of October, salespeople themselves transported the goods from the industrial enterprises and distribution centers to the stores. They used hand carts and, after snow fell, sleds. Often three or four saleswomen would have to haul a valuable load for several hours in going from one end of town to the other. Workers in public catering had their own share of special difficulties. Working in the night to meet a six A.M. deadline, they carried their firewood, water, and provisions by handcart or on their backs without once having a meal delayed. Mostly it was women who worked the stores and dining rooms, many of them replacing men sent to the front. They acquitted themselves with honor in work that demanded great physical endurance and a capacity to be flexible in arranging service for the people. The card system of rationing made additional demands on personnel of the stores. After the strain of the working day, when the stores were closed, there was still the long work of counting coupons. Little time was left for rest, though no one gave this any attention. Everyone's mind was concentrated on delivering goods on schedule or preparing food in time for the following day—no easy matters. The salespeople contributed in no small degree to the general cause of defending the city by doing their work so well.

In September, enemy aircraft sank several barges loaded with grain in Lake Ladoga near the shore at Osinovets. The barges were raised in October by diving crews of the Baltic Fleet. Because of the long immersion, the grain had sprouted. Under normal conditions, it could have been used only as cattle feed; even this grain, however, was very valuable at the time. The grain snatched from Lake Ladoga's fish increased the city's food resources by 2,800 tons. The grain was dried out at the beer breweries, milled again, and mixed with good flour.

By October 20 the supply of barley flour was completely exhausted, and the admixture for rye flour had to be altered. From this date, bread was baked in the following composition: rye flour, 63 per cent; flax cake, 4 per cent; bran, 4 per cent; oat flour, 8 per cent; soya flour, 4 per cent; malt flour, 12 per cent; flour from the moldy grain, 5 per cent. The flavor of this bread was impaired; it reeked of mold and malt.

Two weeks after the change in the formula the question arose again: what to do? The malt flour was now running out and the remaining supplies of rye flour would not permit the percentage of rye in the bread to be raised any further. The search for substitutes went on. A group of workers at the commercial harbor suggested using cottonseed-oil cake as food. A quantity of it had been sent to the harbor in peacetime from the Leningrad oil plant. It had been destined for burning in ship furnaces as it contained a certain amount of down and could not be used for other purposes.[11] Cottonseed-oil cake had never been used as food before. It was believed that it contained a poisonous substance (gossypol) that was injurious to health. Experiments were made, and the fears were found to be groundless. High temperature eliminated the poisonous substance during the process of baking, and there was no further danger. The proposal of the workers was adopted, the new admixture increasing the supply of bread by four thousand tons. The oil cake was immediately transported from the harbor, milled, and used. At first only 3 per cent cottonseed-oil cake was added to the rye flour; after five or six days, however, the amount was raised to 10 per cent. Necessity makes inventors, and thus cottonseed-oil cake became a food for humans.

The utilization of a variety of substitutes in bread-making and the frequent changes in the admixtures, particularly, complicated work in the bread factories and placed a great strain on the employees. A satisfactory quality of the bread was achieved only through the efficient organization of workers, foremen, and laboratory assistants, and the high standards they stood for. In any case, the taste of the bread was as good as the specific admixtures and the quality of the flour allowed. Much credit for efficient management of the bread factories belonged to the director of the Bakery Trust, N. A. Smirnov. Kept busy all the time, he performed his difficult duties with enthusiasm and with good sense, which is more important. Overburdened as he was with immediately pressing problems, he had the ability to foresee impending difficulties and to prepare things for them, averting the many misfortunes which threatened factories from all sides.

These expedients reduced the daily consumption of flour by 1,200 tons. If more than two thousand tons a day were being consumed at the beginning of September, by November 1 the amount had been reduced to 880 tons. This significant saving over the course of forty-five days was the result of the drastic, decisive actions of the Military Council and party and Soviet organizations. By stretching the small supply of bread over a longer period the defenders were winning time. The saving achieved,

[11] At that time the Leningrad oil plant had no lint machines to remove down, and the seeds were processed without cleaning.

however, was only the first step in the battle for food supplies, for peoples' lives.

The organized search for supplementary sources of nourishment concentrated itself in the City Party Committee. Every day advice reached the City Party Committee from different organizations, enterprises, and individuals who suggested ways of producing one sort of foodstuff or another with minimum expenditure of scarce supplies. Every suggestion was carefully examined, as the members of the City Party Committee strongly supported this activity on the part of the citizens. The secretary of the City Party Committee, P. G. Lazutin, devoted a great deal of his effort to organizing the production of food substitutes and working out the system of supply. His reasonableness and intimate knowledge of production techniques helped employees in food and supply to solve their complicated problems. He was the first to appreciate the initiative of scientists attached to a number of scientific institutes in performing experiments to learn whether cellulose could be used for food.

A large quantity of cellulose, originally intended for paper factories, was on hand at the harbor. A group of specialists headed by Professor V. I. Sharkov undertook to devise a method of hydrolyzing the cellulose by means of which it might be transformed into an edible and utilized as an admixture to bread. The institutes worked long and laboriously to find the complicated and then unknown process by which cellulose could be made edible; many a sleepless night was passed before the desired objective was achieved.

The City Party Committee followed the work with strained attention. Especially Lazutin, its secretary, gave full support to the group of scientists in their fine work. The institutes working on the conversion of wood into edible cellulose and later the factories that prepared it received unlimited amounts of current, despite the city's difficulties in obtaining electricity.

Edible cellulose was finally brought forth at the alcohol hydrolysis plant and the Stepan Razin Brewery. The long-awaited cellulose began to arrive at the bread factories at the end of November. From then on bread was made following the recipe: edible cellulose, 10 per cent; cottonseed-oil cake, 10 per cent; chaff, 2 per cent; flour sweepings and dust shaken out of flour sacks, 2 per cent; corn flour, 3 per cent; and rye flour, 73 per cent. The bread factories converted their operations to baking in molds, and the excess weight of a loaf (considered in relation to the amount of flour used in it) reached 68 per cent. The bread was attractive to the eye, white with a reddish crust. Its taste was rather bitter and grassy. The cellulose flour imparted the whiteness to the bread and the bitter taste at the same time. Of course, cellulose was not bran or oil cake or even flour dust from a mill; in combination with other admixtures, however, it was useful. Yeast and yeast milk were produced from the cellulose also, by means of another special process. Leningraders who survived the blockade remember very well the yeast soups which were prepared in almost all the dining rooms. A plate of this soup was often all the food thousands of people received in a day. That supply of cellulose and the ingenuity of the scientists significantly helped the besieged through the hunger.

The City Party Committee selected several hundred Communists to search for food. On instructions of the Military Council, they ransacked every nook and cranny of the vast city—cellars, freight cars, barges, warehouses, wherever food might be found for any of the many reasons resulting from the blockade. Whatever could be used, they noted and had hauled to the warehouses. They took up the floors of the malt houses in the breweries, where they collected 110 tons of malt. Layers of flour dust had been accumulating for years on the walls and floors of the flour mills. In the course of several days the dust was carefully collected, processed, and then used in baking bread. Collectors shook and beat every sack that had ever contained flour. The powder obtained was sifted and used as an admixture. At the commercial harbor there were 2,000 tons of sheep gut. It had been sent there in peacetime for export; all of it was used for food. In freight cars that had been shunted onto sidings one thousand tons of flax-seed cake, five hundred tons of flour, one hundred tons of codfish in barrels, and thirty tons of animal oil were found. In the suburbs, at the state farms, in factories, on river barges, in railroad warehouses there was food, here by the kilogram, there by the ton. They gathered food everywhere, like bees, transported it to the trade depots, processed it, and distributed it according to the plan.

From the start of the blockade until the end of December, 1941, over 18,000 tons of food substitutes, not counting malt, barley, oat, and corn flour, were found, prepared, and eaten. The substitutes consisted mostly of cotton, hemp, cocoa, and flax-seed cake, barley and rye bran, flour-mill dust, cellulose, sprouted grain, rice hulls, corn shoots, cellulose sweepings, bran chaff, and the powder that was beaten out of flour sacks. Those bread substitutes provided more than twenty-five days supply for the population and the troops at a critical time. The seed-cake flour went to the dining rooms, where patties or thick pancakes were made from it, and to the candy factories for further production of candies. Instead of cereals, a grey-black macaroni with a rough surface— made of rye flour with an admixture of 5 per cent flax-seed cake —was often issued. There is no need to describe its taste; the sense of taste had been lost. Thought was concentrated on only one thing: any sort of food to appease the hunger. From oat bran, jelly was made; and soup was prepared from yeast in the dining rooms. It counted on the ration cards as part of the cereal ration.

Attention turned to the fact that two tons of vegetable oils were used every day for greasing the molds for the baking of bread. In view of the critical shortage of fats, such an outlay was extravagant. The bakery laboratories were instructed to find substitutes, and they did. The best substitute turned out to be an emulsion composed of sunflower oil, 20 per cent; soap stock, 4 per cent;[12] corn flour, 1.5 per cent; second-grade wheat flour, 3.5 per cent; and water, 71 per cent. The bread could be removed perfectly well after baking in molds greased with this emulsion. The bread crust did have a strange color, and there was a slightly bitter taste caused by the presence of soap stock. The qualitative flaws were quite bearable; the oil thus saved went to the dining rooms.

At the beginning of October, the City Executive Committee decreed that economic organizations and military units must turn in

[12] A by-product of distilling petroleum, containing fatty acids and oils.

horses not able to work at collecting points of the Leningrad Meat and Dairy Products Market at Kolomyagy and Porokhovye. The horses were not to be slaughtered at places where they were owned. A veterinary inspection at the collecting points decided the suitability of the horsemeat for use as food. Sausage was made from the horsemeat and sold as meat. It was made according to a simple recipe of 75 per cent horsemeat; 12 per cent potato flour; and 11 per cent pork; to this saltpeter, black pepper, and garlic were added. This sausage was excellent in appearance and taste. Horsemeat and sausage counted fully against the ration; there could be no question of prejudice against it. There were not many horses in the city, and horsemeat soon became as rare as pork and other meats. Soya flour in strengths up to 40 per cent was used as an admixture in sausage. Though every means was used to conserve meat and all sorts of substitutes were tried, the supply daily melted away. A meat jelly was concocted out of sheep gut. It gave off such a strong, unpleasant smell that oil of cloves, whose aromatic scent covered the smell of the guts, had to be added. This meat jelly was sold in place of meat at a ratio of 1 to 3; that is, on coupons for one hundred grams of meat one could receive three hundred grams of meat jelly. A small quantity of calf skins was found in the tannery warehouses. Meat jelly was made from the fleshy side of the skins; its taste and smell were revolting, but the defect did not matter. Jellies were made from seaweed also: laminaria and Ahnfeltia. It would be difficult, in fact, to recount all the ingenuity of the Leningraders in finding substitutes for food. Need taught them much.

At this time the matter of food supply resolved itself in two basic problems: first, to set up as quickly as possible a system of mass transportation of freight across the lake and, until food began to arrive, to make the resources on hand last as long as possible in order to prevent leaving the troops and population entirely without food; second, to distribute food in such a way as to restore human energies expended during the working day to some extent, at least for those classes of workers whose labor would decide the fate of the defense.

When it is a question of distributing food, one must not think that it is only a matter of distributing it fairly; this distribution must be regarded as a method, an instrument, a means for increasing production. State support in terms of food must be given only to those workers who are really necessary for the utmost productivity of labor, and if the distribution of food is to be used as an instrument of policy then use it to reduce the number of those who are not unconditionally necessary and to encourage those who are.[13]

These words, spoken by V. I. Lenin many years ago (at the Third All-Russian Food Conference in 1921), under other circumstances and in another situation, were fully applicable to the conditions under which the deadly battle with the enemy was taking place in 1941.

Soon it became necessary to revise the ration quotas even for the basic labor force. The first of the two problems had priority over the second for a long time. There were days when everything hung by a hair and the danger that it would snap loomed like the sword of Damocles over the heads of the besieged. Everything humanly possible was done, in view of the situation, to supply food. Still, it became necessary more and more to reduce rations, to the detriment of many people's health.[14]

[13] V. I. Lenin, *Works*, XXXII, 425.

[14] The products of industry were not so vitally necessary to the besieged as foodstuffs; in the interests of brevity, therefore, my account will confine itself to the Leningraders' struggle to secure food.

4

DISTRIBUTION OF FOOD

August–December, 1941

THE SOVIET GOVERNMENT called millions of people to the colors when the armed forces of Fascist Germany attacked. The most active part of the population was torn away from productive work. Simultaneously, the need for centralized distribution of food and clothing greatly increased. Under these conditions, the government was compelled to introduce a system of rationing in order to make sure that the troops and the urban population received supplies without interruption.

In July, 1941, official food ration quotas were established for the populations of Moscow and Leningrad and their suburbs. The entire urban population of the country was put on a ration system for bread and sugar in August and September. In October the sale of meat products, fats, fish products, cereals, and macaroni was placed on a rationed basis, and from the beginning of the following year numerous industrial products were also rationed. The ration quotas were fixed both with regard to the availability of specific foods and the nature and importance of the work performed by different groups among the population. The fundamental principle of distribution was more food for "shock work" in production. Special ration cards and coupons allowed additional food to men who worked underground or in foundries and at other kinds of hard labor, to blood donors, invalids, pregnant women, and children. In the face of difficult conditions the Soviet state managed to provide the army and urban population with food and industrial products throughout the war. The amount of food permitted on the ration was issued in full, and food prices, like the prices of those basic industrial goods that were rationed, remained at their prewar level throughout the war.

The German conquest of the Ukraine, White Russia, and several *oblasts* of the RSFSR immensely increased the difficulties of supplying the population with food. Nevertheless, the average adult daily ration in the cities did not fall below 2,555 calories in 1942 and increased considerably in the following years. It should be pointed out, however, that it would have been impossible to maintain such a stable level of food supply over a prolonged period of military operations had the system of small, individual farms not been transformed at the propitious moment into collectives using progressive methods on a large scale. The collective farms met their quotas of agricultural products for delivery to the state strictly and efficiently. Testifying to a high degree of readiness to serve their fatherland, the collective farms and collective farmers frequently cut their own requirements in the efforts to supply the needs of the army and industrial centers.

A substantial role in increasing the food resources of the country was played by auxiliary farming on the part of industrial enterprises. The area under crops of these auxiliary farms increased from 3,372,915 acres in 1940 to 7,669,984 acres in 1943.[1] The amount of their cattle was increased several times over. As a rule, produce from the auxiliary farms went to the cafeterias and dining rooms of the industrial enterprises. Public catering increased sharply during the war. Its percentage of the total retail trade in food rose from 13 per cent in 1940 to 25 per cent in 1943. The introduction of food rationing also caused a broad development of vegetable gardening among the urban population. The number of people involved rose from five million in 1942 to 18.6 million in 1945. The area under cultivation in these vegetable gardens more than tripled in size.

[1] See N. Voznesensky, *The War Economy of the USSR during the Fatherland War* (Moscow: State Political Publishing House, 1948), p. 124. The acreage figures are conversions from the hectares given in the original.— Ed.

Recalling the war years, one cannot but admire the people's high degree of self-discipline. Factory workers, collective farmers, office workers, and housewives actively combated speculators and helped the organs of state authority in getting the machinery of distribution moving smoothly, in organizing a wide network of public eating places, and in numerous other ways which made possible the efficient shift on a national scale from free commodity circulation to a rationed economy.

After the shift to the ration system, the inhabitants of Soviet cities obtained food products over and above what they received on their ration cards from the markets of the collective farms and in certain stores. But this was not possible in Leningrad, especially during the first period of the blockade. The sole means of receiving food was the ration card. If a person held an extra ration card by some miracle, he had an incomparable advantage over others. For this reason egotists and sharpers, of whom there were many in so large a city, tried by every means to obtain two, three, or even more cards. For the sake of their stomachs they tried to get ration books, even if it cost the lives of their nearest and dearest. Such people are like locusts. Unless measures can be applied to nip their harmful activities at the very beginning, they are dangerous.

The ration cards that were issued by mistake or obtained by deception caused extra food to be expended, which, under the conditions of siege, was like a stab in the back. The public's confidence in the officials and organizations supervising the distribution of food was undermined. But the egotists (in the worst sense) cared nothing for the fate of the city and its people; they were interested only in themselves. They forged false papers for which they could obtain additional ration cards. They invented a great variety of ways to procure cards illegally: house managers sometimes conspired with janitors to obtain cards for imaginary tenants; the ration cards of dead or evacuated persons would frequently be taken by dishonest employees in the house-manager's office or at the person's place of employment where the cards had been turned in. The efforts to get food by illegal means were live-

ly and aggressive; every administrative slip in recording and issuing ration cards was exploited.

The markets of the collective farms were bare. The population
knew there was no food and nowhere it could come from; the only
plentiful thing was misfortune, which no one was buying because
everyone had enough of his own. Still, in the mornings, a great
number of people would collect at the markets, hoping that
through a stroke of fortune they might find something more for
their stomachs. Sometimes a lucky individual managed to buy a
small package of some kind of tea or a horse bone of doubtful
freshness at a fabulous price. Even such purchases were rare;
there was no food. The ration card was the only source of nutri-
ment. It was more valuable than money, for without it food could
not be obtained. Thus, the issuing of ration cards, keeping them,
recording them, and canceling the coupons were things to be
performed with the same or greater strictness as is observed
in issuing currency. At the beginning of September, however, a
number of *raion* executive committees were giving scant attention
to the workings of the quite complicated and unwieldy machinery
of distribution. In violation of instructions, special coupons for
obtaining food, good only once, were issued. Insufficient care was
exercised to make sure that cards were turned in when their own-
ers lost their rights to them (through being drafted or being assigned to a mess, etc.), and this led to extra consumption of food.
In September seventy thousand coupons for obtaining a single
food ration once were issued by the ration-book offices of the
raion soviets, and a large number of these coupons went to citizens with ration cards. In a number of enterprises workers' rations
were allotted to office workers. Numerous cards were issued to
children who lived outside the city limits of Leningrad. Besides
these, there were other violations, and, if such things were imper-
missible in the ordinary functioning of the distribution system,
they were dangerous in a state of siege. Every ton of food unneces-
sarily consumed directly affected the interests of the population
and the ability of the city to resist. At the beginning of October
the Military Council forbade the issue of special food coupons and
ordered the Leningrad Executive Committee to issue ration cards

to citizens only after carefully examining their papers; to bring to trial those officials who permitted breaches in the regulations concerning the issue of cards; to reinforce the ranks of those engaged in checking ration cards in enterprises and living quarters with the best people from the active membership of the *raion* soviets; and to forbid the managers of enterprises and institutions to dismiss or transfer to other work those engaged in checking ration cards without the consent of the *raion* soviets. More than 3,000 workers from the party and the soviets were assigned in October to supervise the process of registering the papers of those applying for ration cards.

The measures taken to assure strict compliance with the rules for issuing ration cards brought tangible results. In October 2,421,000 cards were issued (not counting the suburbs), or 97,000 fewer than in September. The swindlers who tried to find ways of obtaining cards illegally ran up against such a barrier of public and state vigilance that their activities were paralyzed. A few of the more active ones, to be sure, found ways of acquiring food fraudulently; with the right kind of paper and ink, they printed false ration cards by hand. In stores lit by the flickering light of oil lamps or dim electric lighting, the forgeries passed for genuine. In November the police arrested a woman who had one hundred ration cards in her possession. An office worker in a plant that printed cards for the main city ration-book office, she had managed to steal them and sneak them out of the plant. Other cases of misuse were discovered, and the offenders were severely punished.

The city authorities and the agencies of supply feared that the Fascists might circulate forged ration cards to create confusion, if only for a short time. In a matter like this, involving millions of human lives, a panic could have grave consequences, all the more serious because the enemy was at the gates. It would be easy to drop forged cards from aircraft, and it would be too late to take action after the situation had arisen. The population had to be protected against the danger in advance.

On October 10, the City Executive Committee passed a resolution proposed by A. A. Zhdanov: "In order to stop misuses of ration cards and to prevent the possibility of receiving food supplies by forged ration cards, a reregistration of all cards issued for the month of October will be carried out from October 12 through October 18."

To carry out this reregistration in the middle of the month in so large a city was, even technically, a complicated problem. It required, first of all, a great many people at a time when every worker was needed at his post. The local party organization, nevertheless, assigned over 3,000 Communists to perform this important task. The reregistration took place in house-managers' offices and at places of work. Each citizen had to present documentary proof of his right to a ration card. The documents presented were checked against the actual facts about family and place and nature of work. The cards which survived this process were stamped "Reregistered." Food could not be obtained at the stores after October 18 without the stamp, while ration cards which had not been reregistered were confiscated on presentation. The system provided that coupons were clipped from the cards by sales people in the stores or by waiters in the dining rooms. In all, the number of ration cards for bread decreased by 88,000; for meat products, by 97,000; for fats, by 92,000; and by about the same amount for other products. The decrease occurred chiefly in connection with people who ate at messes but who had failed for one reason or another to turn in their cards at the ration-book offices. Another factor was the removal from circulation of cards that had been obtained by fraud for non-existent persons. How many forged cards disappeared it is hard to say, since no one dared to present them for registration.

The reregistration proved completely justified. Even the skeptics who originally considered it a needless precaution were forced to admit that it had great preventive and practical effect.

At the end of December there occurred an unpleasant surprise. In front of the *raion* ration-book offices long lines began to form of people seeking new ration cards for those they had lost, and the number of losses increased daily. In October 4,800 replacements for lost cards had been issued, in November 13,000, while in December the number rose to 24,000. Here there was cause for thought. Many if not all of the lost cards were found by other people who procured food with them, thus doubling individual food expenditures. The number of citizens "losing" their cards was now snowballing, and prompt intervention in this very unhealthy and dangerous process was required. But how to proceed? To apply the official legal penalty and refuse to replace the lost ration cards would be cruel; those who lost their cards and received no replacements were condemned to the pangs of hunger. The usual disciplinary measures did not seem applicable under the circumstances, since the victims could not buy food for any amount of money. The secretary of the City Party Committee, Kapustin, and the chairman of the City Executive Committee, Popkov, insisted on continuing to replace lost ration cards while requiring the ration-book offices to conduct a careful investigation of the reasons for the loss in every individual case and refuse to issue a new card in the absence of valid evidence. But the chief difficulty lay precisely in the impossibility of establishing that the loss had really taken place. All the victims told about the same story: "I lost my cards while taking cover from the bombing or the artillery fire." If the house had been destroyed, they might add: "The card was in the apartment and the house was wrecked." Many people, of course, did meet with misfortune and their explanations were true, but smart operators had their dirty hands in here too, trying to profit by the miseries of their fellow citizens. Artillery shelling, bombings, fires were everyday occurrences in the city; there was no shortage of good reasons to explain the loss of a ration card, and in practice it proved impossible to distinguish a genuine loss from a pretended one. Thus, having weighed the circumstances, the Military Council decided to discontinue the practice of issuing the new ration cards through the *raion* soviets. A replacement could be issued in exceptional cases, but only through the main city ration-book office. Such a decision, aimed at curtailing abuses and strengthening discipline in matters of supply, was called for by stern necessity. Soon losses dropped sharply and after some time became negligible. Each citizen preserved his ration card very carefully.

In the public dining rooms until the middle of September, coupons were clipped from the diners' ration cards only for meat and bread and only for 50 per cent of the actual amount that went into the preparation of the meal; that is, if one hundred grams of meat were used in the first and second courses, fifty grams' worth was clipped from the card. During the second half of September the authorities began to clip coupons for all the meat and bread consumed, except in a small number of dining rooms of the closed type (at the defense plants). Deductions were not made for other products served in the dining rooms, which was a great help to those who ate there. The number of people who wanted to use these facilities increased daily, as a result of which the *raion* executive committees opened more than three hundred to serve the population, but the available supplies did not permit the system of uncharged food to last very long. In November and December it became necessary to count cereals, macaroni, cheese, sugar, fats, and other products on the ration card.

Ration cards for October and following months were printed in a somewhat revised form adapted to smaller amounts of food, with coupons for twenty-five grams of meat, ten grams of fats, twenty-five grams of cereals and bread, fifty grams of sugar and confectionery. For a meat sandwich weighing fifty grams two coupons were clipped from the ration card: one for twenty-five grams of bread and one for twenty-five grams of meat.

Bread was on sale, in amounts fixed in accord with the established ration quotas, every day. The purchaser had the right to buy his ration one day in advance, but it was categorically forbidden to issue a ration due on a previous day. The sale of foods that were on monthly ration quotas was authorized on each occasion by a special decision of the Military Council. The population was informed by the publication of a decree from the trade department of the Leningrad Executive Committee announcing the amounts of this or that food to be issued during the next ten days. The monthly ration was divided into three parts, not always equal. For example, a worker's card called for 1,500 grams of meat per month, but 400 grams might be sold during the first ten-day period, 500 grams during the second, and 600 during the third. The amount sold during each ten-day period depended on the available supplies, and sometimes the issue of a particular food had to be postponed from one month to the next.

During September and October the established ration quotas were issued promptly; in November, with delays and interruptions, especially in the ration quotas of cereals, fats, and meat. Table 5 shows how food was issued in December.

TABLE 5

MEAT AND MEAT PRODUCTS (In Grams)

Category	Monthly Ration	First Ten Days	Second	Third
Workers and Engineering-Technical Personnel	1500	400	500	600
Office Workers	800	200	300	300
Dependents	400	100	150	150
Children under 12	400	100	150	150

It should be pointed out, however, in order to avoid creating a false impression, that meat, including horse meat, was largely replaced by powdered eggs, meat-vegetable canned goods, and other products, according to the following ratio:

For 1 kilogram of meat—1 kilogram of fish or meat-vegetable canned goods

For 1 kilogram of meat—750 grams of canned meat

For 1 kilogram of meat—2 kilograms of subproducts of second- or third-category meat (heads, feet, lungs, spleen)

For 1 kilogram of meat—3 kilograms of meat jelly or vegetable-and-blood sausage

For 1 kilogram of meat—170 grams of powdered eggs
300 grams of salt pork

Of course, 170 grams of powdered eggs were not equivalent to one kilogram of meat. Had meat been available, few people indeed would have wanted the exchange, but since it was not available, people had to take powdered eggs, jelly made from sheep guts, and vegetable-and-blood sausage: in a word, whatever the stores had on hand.

For butter an equal weight of vegetable oil, condensed milk, salt pork, or lard could be substituted; or in place of one kilogram of butter, 1.5 kilograms of cheese or two kilograms of sour cream could be obtained. In November, but particularly in December, there was neither butter nor its substitutes. It was anticipated that the fats that could not be supplied in December would be made up in January for all categories of ration cards, but in January this could be done only partially, owing to failures in delivery.

TABLE 6

FATS (In Grams)

Category	Monthly Ration	First Ten Days	Second	Third
Workers and Engineering-Technical Personnel	600	....	350	....
Office Workers	250	....	150	....
Dependents	200	....	100	....
Children under 12	500	150	150	200

TABLE 7

CEREALS AND MACARONI (In Grams)

Category	Monthly Region	First Ten Days	Second	Third
Workers and Engineering-Technical Personnel	1,500	300	500	....
Office Workers	1,000	200	350	....
Dependents	600	200	200	....
Children under 12	1,200	300	400	500

TABLE 8

SUGAR AND CONFECTIONERY (In Grams)

Category	Monthly Ration	First Ten Days	Second	Third
Workers and Engineering-Technical Personnel	1,500	500	500	500
Office Workers	1,000	350	350	300
Dependents	800	250	250	300
Children under 12	1,200	400	400	400

For the cereals ration, rye flour with a 50 per cent admixture of flax cake was issued during each second ten-day period.

Children received all foods allotted them on their rations in full and on time.

The general population was supplied with sugar and confectionery promptly and in the prescribed amounts. It is worth noting that no sugar was delivered to Leningrad from the start of the blockade until January, 1942. On September 12 there was enough sugar to last sixty days, but these supplies were made to last more than 110 days. This can be explained by the restrictions placed on the use of sugar (making ice cream, fruit drinks, etc., was prohibited); moreover, the amount of sugar supplied to cafeterias and dining rooms was reduced. Thus it became possible to make sure that the population would receive full rations of sugar and confectionery over a longer period of time.

To give a better idea of the food situation in November and December, 1941, the percentage of the population in each ration category is given:

Worker's Ration:	34.4 per cent of total population of Leningrad
Office-Worker's Ration:	17.5 per cent of total population of Leningrad
Dependent's Ration:	29.5 per cent of total population of Leningrad
Child's Ration:	18.6 per cent of total population of Leningrad

As these figures indicate, two-thirds of the townspeople were on the "hungriest" rations.

So abnormal a relation between the percentage of those drawing worker's rations and the rest is explained by the fact that released workers were reduced to the status of dependents or office workers when industrial plants ceased operating owing to lack of raw materials and the shortage of electricity. In 1943, when coal deliveries to the city increased and factory chimneys began to smoke again, the proportion of workers' ration cards rose to 70 per cent. But in December, 1941, the pulse of Leningrad's industrial life was barely beating. One after the other, plants and factories were closing. And to this calamity affecting the defense of the city and all who lived in it was added the other misfortune: the ration quotas of the discharged workers were cut in half. It would have been only fair to maintain their workers' ration, but the reason that led to the closing of the plants similarly prevented the maintenance of the higher ration level.

The reregistration of ration cards in the middle of the month and counting them by canceled coupons had helped, but still control was complicated, unwieldy, and incomplete. From December on, a change was made in the method of issuing food. Citizens were assigned in equal numbers, and according to their wishes, to specific stores. Foods were sold only to those individuals whose ration cards bore the stamp of the particular store. This procedure made it possible to know how many cards were presented every day to obtain food, which was very important under the circumstances; besides this, the new method made it possible to deliver food to the stores in carefully calculated amounts, an extremely important matter for the agencies of supply in view of their limited resources. Under the new system the citizens received their food without unnecessary fuss and trouble (assuming the food was on hand). This way of issuing food had its inconveniences too, but since its advantages were greater still, it was maintained until the end of the blockade.

From the time ration cards were introduced, the bread ration was repeatedly lowered until December 25, 1941, after which it was gradually increased. The changes in the bread ration can be seen from the figures in Table 9 (in grams per day).

The amounts issued of other rationed foodstuffs changed less often, as may be seen from the data in Table 10 (in grams per month).[2]

It should not be concluded from these figures, however, that the population received the stipulated amounts of meat, cereals, and fats in full measure all the time. Because the table shows only the current official quotas, such a claim would be erroneous; starting in November, the actual issue of food, as pointed out

[2] There were other changes, but these were negligible and temporary.

above, depended on the availability of supplies. In actual fact very little was delivered in November and December or even in January, so that the population often received less than the officially established amounts of food.

In concluding this chapter on food distribution, it should be noted that the imposition of one ration on children of all ages was not justified in practice. Children over ten needed a ration different from that of the three- to six-year-old group both in kind and quantity of food. Young people from twelve to fourteen received only "dependent's" rations, although their bodies required

TABLE 9

Type of Card	July	Sept. 2	Sept. 12	Oct. 1	Nov. 13	Nov. 20	Dec. 25	Jan. 24, 1942	Feb. 11, 1942
Workers......	800	600	500	400	300	250	350	400	500
Office Workers	600	400	300	200	150	125	200	300	400
Dependents...	400	300	250	200	150	125	200	250	300
Children under 12.........	400	300	300	200	150	125	200	250	300

TABLE 10

	Workers and Engineering-Technical Personnel	Office Workers	Dependents	Children under 12
*Meat**				
From July to September..........	2,200	1,200	600	600
From September to January, 1942..	1,500	800	400	400
Cereals and Macaroni				
From July to September..........	2,000	1,500	1,000	1,200
From September to February, 1942.	1,500	1,000	600	1,200
Fats				
From July to September..........	800	400	200	400
From September to November.....	950	500	300	500
From November to January, 1942..	600	250	200	500
Sugar and Confectionery				
From July to September..........	1,500	1,200	1,000	1,200
From September to November.....	2,000	1,700	1,500	1,700
From November to January, 1942..	1,500	1,000	800	1,200

* From July to September fish was also issued.

a more nourishing diet. The situation made it impossible to give them better food.

A description of the system of distributing food would be incomplete without mention of the people who created it and assured its operation. As a rule, the organization of supply and the quotas to be issued were worked out by the joint efforts of the administration, trade specialists, and the community. The supply workers, in whatever sectors they found themselves, large or small, displayed exceptional qualities of discipline and exactingness, especially in overcoming their own hunger. Bearing full responsibility for the problems confronting them, they did their duty painstakingly, finding good solutions to innumerable difficulties. By selfless work and initiative, they regularly found new and better ways to distribute food and daily strove to serve the besieged population more efficiently. What sort of people were they, who honorably lived up to the high confidence placed in them? They were mostly young people—Comsomol members, people singled out by the production collectives, by party, Soviet, and trade-union organizations for the hard labor of supply under conditions of acute shortage in all kinds of provisions. I. A. Andreenko, the director of the city trade department, devoted much effort to organizing the supply service. Endowed with a firm and persevering character, he toiled many hours each day over instructions, regulations, and other tedious but necessary documents concerning the distribution and recording of supplies. Andreenko demanded much from his subordinates and gave no quarter to those who violated the rules of trade. His stern nature was widely known, and he was feared, especially by those who were not against making a little profit on the side if the opportunity occurred. But anyone who knew Andreenko well would say that he demanded more from himself than from anyone else. Holding a responsible post dealing with the distribution of material blessings, he permitted neither himself nor anyone else the least departure from the legally established ration quotas.

The measures taken by the city party organization made it possible to protect the population from speculators, swindlers, and spongers. The inhabitants' confidence in the established system of food distribution was maintained. There was little food, but each individual knew that his ration would not be given to anyone else. He would receive whatever he was supposed to receive.

The period from the middle of November, 1941, to the end of January, 1942, was the worst of the entire blockade. By this time local supplies were exhausted and deliveries across Lake Ladoga were on too small a scale to count. All the hopes and expectations of the people were now directed toward the Winter Road.

5

FOOD FOR THE TROOPS

July–December, 1941

THE PROBLEM OF supplying troops with food is one of paramount importance in all periods of history. The soldier who is limited to a bit of bread and never gets enough to eat loses his fighting qualities. It must be remembered, too, that the numerical size of armies in wartime is now reckoned in the millions of men. To feed such masses, enormous quantities of a variety of foodstuffs are required. A country is not likely to stand the strain unless it practices every possible economy and calculates its ration levels wisely.

This was just what happened in the old Russian army in the First World War, 1914–18. During the first months of war (August–November, 1914), ration quotas for the troops of the field army were set too high: 1,230 grams of bread per man per day; 615 grams of meat, 106 grams of fats, 68 grams of sugar, and 256 grams of vegetables. These rations of basic foods were not necessary (aside from vegetables) and were larger than a soldier's normal requirements. This amounted to a squandering of state resources, including food, and at the beginning of 1916, in the second year of war, the country began to feel the pinch of a food shortage. The military authorities decreased the meat ration by two-thirds and the fats ration by more than one-half. The new amounts per day were 205 grams of meat and 42 grams of fats. By the end of 1916 the problems of food supply had become still more acute. The ration quotas for bread, sugar, and cereals were substantially reduced once more, both in the field army and the units in the interior of the country.

While provisions in the areas near the front were exhausted, the feeble rail transportation system was incapable of delivering the amounts necessary even for the reduced ration from inside Russia. The troops suffered. When the small ration of fresh vegetables was not issued for a long period, scurvy affected hundreds of thousands. By the end of the war, the revolting disease had assumed threatening proportions. According to the statistics of the commission to investigate the medical consequences of the war of 1914–17, more than 500,000 soldiers of the field army came down with scurvy in 1916 and the first nine months of 1917 alone.

It is obvious from what has been said that ration quotas for the troops at the beginning of the First World War were set without regard to the productivity of agriculture and industry or the condition and capacity of rail transport. There was, too, an essential defect in the composition of the food ration: the small quantity of vegetables and potatoes (256 grams) neither provided for sufficient variety in the diet nor met the natural individual need for vitamins, leading to serious health disorders among the soldiers.

During the Great Patriotic War of 1941–45, the troops of the field forces as well as units stationed in the zone of the interior were fed according to quotas established by the government on September 20, 1941. The quotas were announced in Order Number 312 of the People's Commissariat of Defense on September 22, 1941. The size and composition of the ration were determined by scientifically based calculations of what was necessary to assure officers and men a full-valued but not excessive diet. Due regard was given to the difficulties in food supply that would result from the enemy's anticipated penetration into the bread-producing regions of the Ukrainian and White Russian republics, the removal of a considerable part of the laboring population from productive labor, and the diversion of tractors, trucks, and other types of equipment from use in agriculture.

The new ration quotas were sharply differentiated: compared to the prewar Red Army ration, those of the combat units were larger and those of the units in the rear areas were smaller. The nutritive value of the various types of rations instituted September 20, 1941, is given in Table 11, which is based on data of the Red Army's Science Research Dietetic Institute.

Early in the war, some modification of the combat ration quotas was made: instead of 150 grams of meat and 100 grams of fish, 180 grams of meat were issued. Otherwise the ration did not change until the end of the war.

In composition, caloric content, and vitamin and mineral content, the ration passed the long test of a grim war. Experience in provisioning the troops showed, however, that including fish in the ration as an essential separate component made no sense. In

TABLE 11

TYPE OF UNITS	AMOUNT IN GRAMS			CALORIC CONTENT
	Protein	Fats	Carbo-hydrates	
Combat Units....................	103	67	587	3,450
Rear of the Field Army............	84	56	508	2,954
Combat and Reserve Units not assigned to the field army..........	87	48	489	2,822
Guard detachments and Rear installations........................	80	48	458	2,659

practice, it turned out to be impossible to supply fish in large enough quantities to the field army to assure its daily issue. Moreover, under war conditions, it is extremely difficult to prepare meals of meat and fish at the same time. Fish should be regarded only as a meat substitute, useful for varying the diet.

In the field army one food was often substituted for another according to a scheme provided for in a special table. This system enabled cooks to vary their menus and made it easier for supply officers to furnish provisions. Such substitutions, however, often reduced the food value of the daily ration. Thus, for instance, according to the table one hundred grams of meat were equivalent to seventeen grams of powdered eggs, whereas, after finishing an omelet instead of a portion of meat, a soldier actually felt that his stomach was still empty. Substituting certain kinds of canned fish for meat also proved inadequate. These and other shortcomings were corrected in the course of the war; in particular, the substitution of powdered eggs for meat was forbidden.

The daily ration of vegetables and potatoes was 820 grams per man. Multiplied by millions of men, this considerable weight constituted an impressive total needed to meet a daily requirement. Especially in winter, transporting and preserving fresh vegetables and potatoes were complicated and difficult matters, for which a large amount of rolling stock had to be diverted from carrying other types of freight; but in return the soldiers enjoyed varied and tasty nourishment. When vegetables could not be supplied over a long time to a certain formation, as a result of the military situation, its officers and men were treated to a prescribed daily dose of a Vitamin C preparation. The soldiers of the Soviet Army did not suffer from scorbutic diseases during the war.

The provisioning of the troops involved in the defense of Leningrad depended directly on the resources available inside the ring of the blockade. These resources were insignificant. If economizing food had been the only consideration, the troop rations would have been cut on the first day of the siege, since they accounted for a large proportion of the total amount of food consumed. This was not ordered because the soldiers and sailors were holding the city's defenses against violent German assault in September. Constant enemy fire and bad autumn weather exhausted the soldiers, and good food rations replenished their strength. It would have been folly to reduce rations at such a time.

In September the troops were fed, as before the siege, according to the food quotas set by the order of the People's Commissariat of Defense on September 22, 1941. As soon as the front was stabilized, however, and the Germans went over to the defensive, the Military Council ordered a cut in the rations of rear units and a small reduction in the amount of vegetables and fish issued to the front-line troops.[1]

---

[1] Besides the ration given here, there were others for the air force, naval forces, etc. For the sake of brevity the ration received by the majority of personnel of the Leningrad Front is the one presented here.

Starting October 1, 1941, the troops of the Leningrad Front received the following ration as listed in Table 12, in grams per day per man.

In a number of sectors during the siege, front-line and rear units were stationed so close to each other that it was hard to tell the rear from the front line. Still the distinction in ration quotas between the two was justified and had the full approval of soldiers and officers.

TABLE 12

	Front-line Troops	Rear Units
Bread......................	800	600
Meat......................	150	75
Fish.......................	80	50
Cereals....................	140	70
Macaroni..................	30	20
Fats, Lard.................	30	20
Vegetable Oil..............	20	20
Sugar......................	35	20
Vegetables and Potatoes.......	500	400
Salt.......................	30	30
Tea.......................	1	1
Spices (Pepper, vinegar, laurel leaves, etc.)................	3	3

TABLE 13

Bread...................	400
Meat...................	50
Fish...................	50
Fats...................	40
Sugar...................	35
Cereals.................	100
Vegetables and Potatoes....	400

The various militarized detachments and formations of civilian departments were taken off soldiers' rations and put on a smaller so-called "militarized guard ration," which consisted of the foods shown in Table 13, in grams per day per man.

When vegetables and potatoes were not available, the troops might be issued cereals instead, at the rate of twenty grams of cereals for one hundred grams of vegetables, but from November on, the substitution was at the rate of ten grams of cereals for one hundred grams of vegetables.

The food was prepared in battalion kitchens and delivered hot to the troops in the front line, usually twice a day, at dawn and again in the evening just after sunset. In the interval between deliveries of hot food, cold lunches were issued: bread, boiled meat, or canned goods, potatoes boiled in the skins, and other edibles. If military conditions prevented the delivery of hot food from the battalion kitchen to some formations, "dry rations" were issued, consisting of foods that required no culinary treatment: hardtack, canned goods, sugar, tea, salt, food concentrates, pea soup purée, wheat or buckwheat porridge. From such a variety of foods the soldiers themselves could easily make a hot meal of two courses in no more than five to seven minutes.

The soldiers and sailors repeatedly expressed their gratitude to the industrial workers for the food concentrates. Concentrates, especially those made from vegetables—*borshch*, cabbage soup, and potato soup, seasoned with spices—made possible a more or less varied diet for the soldiers, even in places occupied by small groups of men where the ubiquitous kitchen could not reach. Produced in the form of lightweight briquets, the concentrates were easy to transport and could be stored safely for a comparatively long time.

Women replaced the Red Army cooks in a number of units. The women had first gone through brief training courses to master the peculiarities of field kitchens and the composition and amounts of the daily ration. The experience of the Great Patriotic War has shown the obvious advisability of substituting female for male labor in mobile field kitchens. Every male soldier is needed in the front line to fight the enemy in time of war. When it is possible to free men from rear duty, even when the rear is near the battle area, the step must be taken, especially when it improves matters. Women prepared the soldiers' meals well; they kept kitchen implements cleaner and handled the food more efficiently; in short, they took their job more deeply to heart and were willing to put more effort into it.

Bread for the troops was usually baked at the city bread factories rather than the military bakeries to permit a better check on consumption and to save flour through large excesses in the weight

of the loaves over that of the flour used in them. Field bakeries
turning out rye bread from a type of flour containing some bran
produced an excess weight of 52 or 53 per cent, while the mechanized bread factories in the city raised this figure for the same
flour to over 60 per cent. Delivering the bread to the troops presented no difficulties, since distances were short and the roads in
good condition.

Ration levels were lowered for both the civilian population and
the troops as supplies decreased. From the middle of November
until February, 1942, the daily ration of a front-line soldier
amounted to 2,593 calories; for the rear units the ration was 1,605

TABLE 14

Type of Troops	Up to Oct. 1			Starting Oct. 1			Starting Nov. 8			Starting Nov. 20		
	Bread	Meat	Fish	Bread	Meat	Fish	Bread	Meat	Fish	Bread	Meat	Fish
Front Line...	800	150	100	800	150	80	600	125	.....	500	125	.....
Rear Units..	700	120	80	600	75	50	400	50	.....	300	50	.....
Hospi- tals....	600	120	50	600	120	50	400	50	.....	300	50	.....

calories, while the civilian population received much less. A sizable difference in rations for people who were all in virtually the
same condition during the siege seemed unjust, but war has its
laws which must not be disregarded. The enemy army, ready to
spring at any moment, was waiting for the defenders' resistance
to weaken. To reduce the rations of the soldiers under these circumstances till they approximated those of the inhabitants meant
bringing the fighting men to the point of exhaustion. If the soldiers' legs had started to buckle from hunger, the city's defense
would have been in dreadful danger, despite all their endurance
and lofty soldierly spirit.

During the blockade the largest reductions in the soldier's rations were made in bread, meat, and fish, as may be seen from
Table 14 (in grams per man per day).

FIG. 1.—Patrol planes guarding Leningrad as the front approaches the city. (Courtesy of Sovfoto.)

Fig. 2.—Citizens and soldiers listening to a communiqué in the summer of 1941. (Courtesy of Sovfoto.)

Fig. 1.—Patrol planes guarding Leningrad as the front approaches the city. (Courtesy of Sovfoto.)

Fig. 2.—Citizens and soldiers listening to a communiqué in the summer of 1941. (Courtesy of Sovfoto.)

Fig. 3.—The preparation of defense works went on all through the summer and winter. (Courtesy of Sovfoto.)

FIG. 4.—Spur-line construction along the Ladoga route. (Courtesy of Sovfoto.)

Fig. 5.—First civilian victims of the German cannonading with long-range guns. (Courtesy of Sovfoto.)

Fig. 6.—The lack of fuel and damage suffered by the electrical systems forced everyone to go on foot. These women are hauling heavy bundles on improvised sledges. (Courtesy of Sovfoto.)

Fig. 7.—"Drive slowly! Unexploded bomb! Danger!" says the notice painted on the fence. In the foreground, children have organized scooter races. (Courtesy of Sovfoto.)

These rations were reduced because of difficulties in delivering provisions to Leningrad. No fish was delivered at all, yet the fish could not be compensated for by the issue of more meat. At the end of January, 1942, the military bread ration was increased, and rations for the other foods were increased later, when some food reserves had accumulated in the city as a result of satisfactory deliveries over the Ice Road.

Besides food, the soldiers and sailors were issued twenty grams of shag (*makhorka*) or ten grams of tobacco per man per day. For the soldier at the front, smokes were indispensable to pass time and overcome the monotony of the dugout. It was frequently noticed that soldiers became bored and gloomy when they had nothing to smoke; they found it easier to miss meals than tobacco, even for a very short time. And now one more misfortune was being added to all the others that had fallen to the lot of the defenders: tobacco supplies were coming to an end. The troops must not be left without smokes even for a short time. All the thoughts of supply and industry were directed toward finding substitutes that could be mixed into the remaining tobacco. At the beer breweries twenty-seven tons of hops were discovered, all of which were used as an admixture (in strength of 10 to 12 per cent) to tobacco. Gradually, dry aspen, birch, oak, maple, and other leaves began to be used as admixtures. Tests of tobacco mixed with each type of leaf showed that maple leaves made the best admixture for smoking. Factory workers and school children collected the leaves, which were dried in the open air, packed in sacks, and taken by military transport to factories where they were added to the tobacco, after technical processing, in proportions up to 20 per cent. About eighty tons of leaves were thus utilized. As a nicotine "seasoning," tobacco dust was collected from under the floors of the tobacco plants and mixed in. Owing to the shortage of paper, the tobacco was not put into packs but into bags weighing as much as twenty kilograms.

V. I. Ionide, chief tobacco foreman at the Uritsky factory, worked hard at devising tobacco substitutes. The right mixture of leaves, hops, and tobacco dust reminded smokers of the taste of real tobacco, thanks to his inventiveness. The successful use of substitutes made it possible to keep the soldiers supplied with smokes at all times.

With a view to economizing tobacco, the supply service was authorized to make the exchange of sweets for tobacco (Table 15) on a soldier's request.

This exchange, however, was unsuccessful. Although the ersatz tobacco crackled like gunpowder in the pipe or home-made paper cigar and left an unpleasant sensation in the mouth, few men wanted to exchange their tobacco ration for chocolate or other confectioneries.

TABLE 15

In place of 300 grams of tobacco, 200 grams of chocolate
In place of 300 grams of tobacco, 300 grams of sugar
In place of 300 grams of tobacco, 300 grams of candy

The supply service must always have stocks of shag (*makhorka*) and tobacco on hand to meet the soldiers' strong craving to smoke. The argument that says, "We need chow; tobacco we can live without," is unacceptable. The question is not one of survival but of the morale and mood of the troops; the experience of the war tells us, whether we like it or not, that this is something to be reckoned with as having real importance.

Arguments similar to those about tobacco can be heard about spices: field kitchens are supposed to be able to get along without spices if there is difficulty in transport. It is true, of course, that seasonings are neither bread nor meat, and nobody's death has been laid to a lack of pepper, laurel leaf, or other spices in his food. But every housewife, nevertheless, considers it necessary to have various condiments on her table; and not from whim. Peoples' taste buds are avid for things that arouse the appetite, and this cannot be overlooked. The supply service of the Soviet Army had difficulty during the war in providing the troop units with spices. Some formations received none for two or three months on end, and this led to loss of appetite among the soldiers. As a matter of fact, such unpretentious dishes as cabbage soup are tasteless without spices and if they are served often, people get sick of them, but only a pinch of black pepper in that same cabbage soup makes it taste much different. The mouth is pleasantly irritated and lost appetite returns; the food is eaten up, the soldiers are satisfied, and satisfied people are in good spirits. This should always be remembered when it comes to providing a soldiers' kitchen with spices.

Fascist Germany, taking into account the lessons of World War I, followed a persistent policy with regard to food of expanding production, controlling consumption, and creating reserves of agricultural products. The well-known Brazilian scholar Josue de Castro has written:

> In order to achieve a total mobilization of food resources the Third Reich as early as 1933 issued a series of special laws. All landowners and owners of enterprises involved in the food industry, wholesale and retail food merchants, were put under the strict supervision of a special agency, the "Reich Administration for Food Problems," which was responsible for leading the nation in a struggle to supply itself adequately with the means of existence. In practice this was done by creating enterprises to produce food substitutes or ersatz products and by preparing the people psychologically; they were put on a war ration a good six years before the first shot was fired.[2]

Just before the war, on August 27, 1939, the German government passed a law requiring compulsory deliveries of agricultural products to the state by the peasants. According to the law, vegetable products were subject to compulsory delivery from the moment of their "separation from the soil," and animal products from the moment they were in hand. A specified amount of grain was left to the peasants for seeding and feeding livestock. For their own nourishment the peasants were allowed to keep the amount of food permitted by the established ration quotas.

In contrast to 1914, Germany had rather large reserves of critical foodstuffs by the beginning of World War II (1939): about

[2] Josué de Castro, *Geography of Hunger* (Foreign Literature Publishing House, 1964), p. 313. De Castro is a historian at the University of São Paulo. He is a Communist.

six million tons of grain and 600,000 tons of fats. Since Germany usually imported about two million tons of grain a year and 400,000 tons of fats, her reserves were enough to last from a year-and-a-half to three years even if imports from outside ceased entirely, assuming normal harvests at home. Sugar needs of the people and the army could be met by German production. Before starting the war with the Soviet Union, the Germans further built up their reserves by plundering Poland, Holland, Norway, Czechoslovakia, and many other countries. Even so, they could not maintain the size of the soldiers' rations at its peacetime level after the war began. Both in quantity of foods supplied and in nutritive value, the ration level had to be lowered. Like a swarm of locusts, the field army of many millions devoured the reserves as well as the meager harvests of the war years, and locusts, as we know, can eat a lot.[3]

Germany went to war with carefully worked out directives on feeding her troops: instead of the two ration levels operative in peacetime—field and rear—three different rations were devised for the war period: the "large ration" for all special-duty units, the "small ration with extras" for reserve and training units and military schools, and the "small ration" for all other units, staffs, and services.

The size of each of these rations per man, beginning May 15, 1939, is given in Table 16.

While the soldiers' peacetime rations contained 3,507 calories, from the beginning of the war (in the field forces) it consisted of 3,236 calories. Despite accumulated reserves, the Germans consumed their food supplies cautiously, recalling the First World War when the population was fed on yellow turnip soup beginning with the winter of 1916–17, and hunger caused considerable illness. Thus, at the zenith of its power, on June 20, 1941, the Fascist Reich again reduced the ration, to 2,750 calories, by cutting the amount of bread 100 grams, meat 70 grams, sugar

[3] According to the figures of the German general, A. Weidemann, the German armed forces totaled 10.2 million men in July, 1944, which is about nine times more than in peacetime (*Lessons of the Second World War* [Moscow: Foreign Literature Publishing House, 1957], p. 295).

40 grams, and peas and beans 30 grams. In order to economize still more, Hitler's government sent its troops out "prospecting" for additional foodstuffs in the territories of the foreign states they had seized.

After a year of war with the USSR, the Germans revised their system of provisioning the troops. They introduced new and more differentiated ration levels on July 1, 1942, and brought the ration for combat units down to 2,543 calories. The reduction

TABLE 16

TYPE OF FOOD	AMOUNT IN GRAMS AND CALORIC CONTENT		
	Large Ration	Small with Extras	Small
Rye Bread...............	750	750	650
Meat...................	250	180	150
Canned Meat............	130	130	130
Fats...................	50	30	30
Potatoes...............	1,500	1,500	1,500
or			
Peas, Beans.............	180	180	180
Sugar..................	80	80	80
Coffee.................	10	10	10
Fresh onions...........	10	10	10
Nutritional Composition of the Ration			
Protein................	139	127	118
Fats...................	81	60	58
Carbohydrates..........	465	464	422
Caloric Content........	3,236	2,997	2,785

reflected the Fascist government's anxiety for their country's future, because the war, contrary to plan, was obviously becoming a prolonged affair. At the same time they were well aware that the soldiers would find it hard to live and fight on the reduced ration and that they would fleece the populations of the occupied countries. Exactly this is what happened. An organized plundering took place. In every section of Soviet territory occupied by the enemy, there was appointed a special Fascist commissioner for agriculture, the so-called *"Sonderfuehrer."* In an army rear area these commissioners were subordinated to the staff of the particular army.

Divisional supply officers would transmit requisitions to the *Sonderfuehrers* for amounts of food required by their units. On the basis of this request, the *Sonderfuehrer* would issue a warrant for obtaining provisions from a certain collective farm or grain warehouse. On presentation of the warrant the headman of the collective farm would hand over the specified provisions to the representative of the military unit. By this open pillage of the Soviet population, the German soldiers were actually fed according to their demands and not according to the ration levels. The host of police, commissioners, and *Sonderfuehrers* in the occupied territories grew like thistles in an abandoned farmstead, all doing their best to make off with the peasants' grain, livestock, poultry, vegetables, and potatoes. But the Fascists were not content to feed their army at the expense of the territories they had seized. They ravaged and ransacked several thousand of our collective and state farms and slaughtered, confiscated, or sent to Germany seven million horses, 17 million large horned cattle, 20 million pigs, and 27 million sheep and goats.[4]

Following a set plan, the German army and occupation authorities sent thousands of trains to Germany loaded with plunder from every spot where their armies set foot. From Poland alone during the first two years of war, the Nazi authorities confiscated and exported more than 950,000 tons of grain, 800,000 pigs, 100 million eggs, and many other kinds of provisions. The Polish population, especially in the cities, felt the pangs of hunger, and many people died from a prolonged malnutrition. In fact, this had been precisely the Nazi objective. Methodically they applied a "plan of organized hunger" in the occupied countries. In Greece, after its conquest by the Germans, a famine of catastrophic proportion broke out, taking the lives of many families of workers and peasants. The famine deliberately created was an original weapon for waging war in the arsenal of Hitler's Germany and the Fascists used it widely in the attempt to break all will to resist.

In sentencing the people of occupied countries to the tortures of hunger, the Germans managed to keep the diet of their own

---

[4] See *Nuremberg Trials* (State Juridical Publishing House, 1952), I, 723, 724.

population at about its prewar level during the war years. The diet of the Germans sharply worsened (1,600–1,800 calories), however, as soon as the Fascist hordes were driven out of foreign lands. Still, Germany experienced no serious food problems up to the end, because her military machine was out of commission from the blows of Soviet troops before a food crisis developed.

6

TRANSPORTATION OF SUPPLIES
BY WATER AND AIR

September–November, 1941

A STRETCH of sixty-five kilometers across Lake Ladoga separated the Germans at Schluesselburg from the Finns on the Karelian Isthmus, and it was just this chink that the defenders turned into a supply artery for Leningrad.

From Cape Osinovets to the mouth of the Volkhov River the lake route was open, except for the German air force, which was, during the period September–November, particularly active. The territory directly bordering Lake Ladoga on the south, however, was a front-line sector occupied by the enemy, so that here the water route passed within range of German artillery and was under enemy observation almost all the way. The line of communications had to be created across the Schluesselburg Bay, despite these extremely unfavorable conditions, because there was no other possibility. The new land-water route ran as follows: Leningrad–Osinovets–Novaya Ladoga–Volkhov–Tikhvin–Cherepovets–Vologda. (See Map 4.) Goods for Leningrad reached Volkhov by rail, where they were unloaded and loaded onto docks at Gostinopolye. The cargo then went down the river to its confluence with Lake Ladoga. At Novaya Ladoga the goods were loaded on lake barges, from which they were transferred to the narrow-gauge railroad upon arrival at Osinovets. For the fourth time they were reloaded now onto the freight cars of the main railroad line.

The harbor at Novaya Ladoga was in semi-abandoned condition. It had little mooring space or equipment, no ship cranes, and its access roads were in need of repair. Lake barges, moreover, have to load here at a considerable distance from shore, since their draft does not permit them to enter the mouth of the river. Another handicap, the frequently gusty winds of the fall, interfered with loading and unloading operations and sometimes halted them altogether. Ships moored in the roadway made good targets for enemy aviation, a fact which the Germans exploited, bombing and strafing from the air. Those engaged in the work of loading had nowhere to take cover during the raids. The conditions under which cargoes were delivered were thus painfully difficult, but there was no other route. The extremity of the danger was understood by the thousands who toiled on the Ladoga road, but they also realized clearly the importance of the work to the country and did their duty proudly.

Osinovets, fifty-five kilometers from Leningrad on the Karelian Isthmus, was the point chosen for the construction of the port on the western shore of the lake. Here a thick mixed forest stretched in a broad band along the lake, making it possible to conceal warehouses, cargoes, access roads, anti-aircraft artillery, and machine guns from enemy eyes. Another factor in the choice of this site for the future port was the direct proximity to Osinovets of the Irinovsk Railroad and its last station, Lake Ladoga. Movement of trucks, freight-handling carts, and people from the lake to the station was hidden beneath the domes of giant evergreen pines. There were, however, strong arguments against constructing the port here, for the shore at Osinovets was sandy, low, and sloping, and ships could not approach because of reefs, which increased the difficulties of handling the vessels and forced them to stand off conspicuously. Enemy aviation exploited these conditions and caused much trouble, but the evils and inconveniences were borne since there was not a better place in the land of the besieged.

In relatively short order army units and workers built four large piers for mooring ships, deepened the draft by 70,000 cubic meters of bottom, laid a narrow-gauge railroad from the wharf to the main railroad, built warehouses for food, fuel, and ammu-

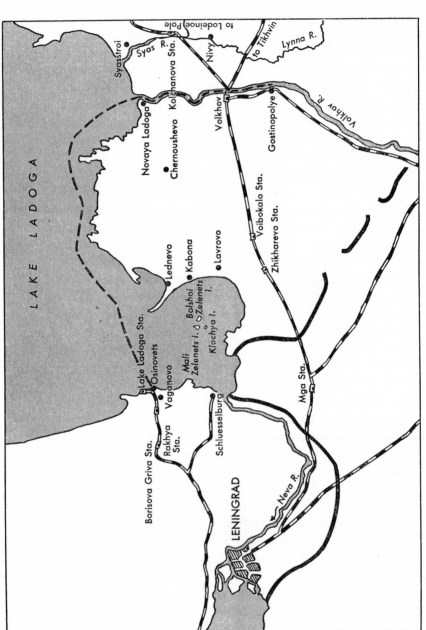

MAP 4.—Supplying Leningrad (September–November, 1941)

nition, and dug bunkers for various naval and security services. From plants in the city and from the Leningrad commercial docks came cranes, freight-handling carts for the narrow-gauge line, and other port machinery and equipment. The construction was carried on efficiently at a high tempo, but months of dogged labor were still necessary to bring into being on a deserted shore the port that substituted for all of Leningrad's railroad stations and sea and river harbors over so considerable a length of time.

In the search for means of transportation, the workers of the river fleet showed considerable skill in improvising. Almost all the lake barges and tugs had been closed off in the Neva, and those that dared run for it were sunk by direct fire from the Germans stationed on the left bank of the river. Of the river barges on the Volkhov, many were unemployable because Ladoga's rough waters would have smashed and sunk them easily. There were, however, twenty or thirty river barges in the backwaters of Novaya Ladoga, left there in peacetime for scrapping as not up to official standards. All hope rested on these discarded craft of another day. With the help of naval personnel, twenty-seven of the barges were reconditioned to carry dry cargoes. Also used for transport were ships of the ladoga naval flotilla.

The first two barges arrived at Osinovets, carrying eight hundred tons of grain, on September 12, 1941. The arrival was a great event that raised the spirits of the besieged, for the population saw the link between the city and the rest of the country and realized that the country was helping. Three days later, five more vessels arrived with three thousand tons of wheat. This time, unfortunately, the grain was not in sacks but had been poured directly into the holds to save time. Workers at the procurement depots in Leningrad *oblast* had been too eager to move the grain, and when sacks were temporarily not available had sent the grain loose without regard for the unusual circumstances prevailing at Osinovets.

To avoid crowding ships in the open roadway in sight of the enemy and to compensate for the shortage of ships by an accelerated "turn-around," port regulations required barges to unload in six hours. Both of these conditions were grossly violated with the arrival of the unpacked grain. Despite the assignment of many extra hands to sack the wheat and unload the barges in the road-way, their departure on the return voyage was delayed. As a re-sult, enemy aircraft sank three of the barges with the grain aboard. In two weeks, however, the vessels had been raised, repaired, and recommissioned, and the grain, which had sprouted in the water, was used to make bread. Of course, the Leningraders had reason to regret the incident, but those who sent the grain felt even worse when they learned the consequences of their hastiness.

Crowds of citizens began to collect along the shore on the fourth day of the operation of the transport route over the lake to Osinovets. They hoped to be ferried to the opposite shore. These were, in large part, people from German-occupied cities such as Pskov and Luga, and from the Latvian and Estonian Soviet republics who had been separated by no fault of their own from their families. Pursued by misfortune, they were now hurrying to seek their loved ones on the other side of the lake. This dis-organized arrival of crowds of people disturbed the work of the port, however, and the Military Council forbade private individu-als entrance to the zone of the harbor. Evacuation was carried out only by special permission at strictly prescribed times.

The enemy was on the alert for traffic over the lake. His aim was to paralyze the shipping by attacking from the air to the limit of his capability. Ships therefore left Osinovets as a rule un-der cover of darkness. But since the crossing to Novaya Ladoga required sixteen hours—the slow tugboats did not get very far during the night—a considerable distance still had to be traversed in daylight. Ship captains executed dizzying maneuvers, often successfully, to avoid the bombs of pursuing aircraft, but some-times ships were lost. One of these tragedies occurred on Novem-ber 4, 1941. The transport *Konstruktor* left Osinovets at night heading for Novaya Ladoga. On board were families being sent to join defense workers who had been previously evacuated to new places of work. By daylight the transport was sighted by a German airplane several miles out of Osinovets. The pilot un-doubtedly saw the unarmed ship clearly, and the women and children on her deck, but began to bomb her nevertheless. By swerving the ship to one side, the captain avoided the air-pirate's first bombs, which went harmlessly to the bottom. On the second run, however, a single bomb struck the ship, piercing the deck and exploding in the hold. One hundred and two people were killed or injured as a result, among them thirty members of the crew. Many women and children were blown overboard by the blast wave into the icy water with no chance of rescue. Holed by the bomb, the ship was now sinking.

A criminal rarely has the chance to watch his victims in their agony, but the crew of the airplane continued to circle at low altitude, and when they spotted people swimming, finished them off with machine-gun fire. By good fortune, a Soviet patrol gunboat arrived on the scene of the catastrophe. Through the heroic efforts of her men, the half-sunken *Konstruktor* was brought into port. For those who witnessed the frightful tragedy, the weeping of the surviving women who lost children in the lake and the groans of the wounded sound to this day. But though death soared over the lake continually, navigation had to go on.

On the decision of the State Defense Committee, the delivery of supplies to Leningrad from the interior of the country came under the direction of the Soviet Army's Rear Services. The best-suited organization for the task, its representatives were in every *oblast,* at railroad stations and large industrial enterprises. Its officers saw to it that the management of plants, factories, mills, and supply bases promptly carried out instructions from headquarters regarding delivery of foodstuffs and other supplies.

With characteristic energy, Commander of the Rear Services, General of the Army A. V. Khrulev, demanded that his staff give top priority to provisions for Leningrad on the basis of his quick, accurate evaluations of the situation developing at the front. An exacting system to control the loading and passage of freight trains was established. Every through freight carried a number in a prescribed series. The progress of these trains was followed by the railroad administration and Military Communications Service. If a train was held up, officers of the Military Communications Service and railroad men took steps on the spot to remove the obstacle and send the train on. Under such a well-organized delivery system, food trains arrived continually at Volkhov Station despite numerous hindrances. From here the loads were transported to the river port of Gostinopolye, located nine kilometers from Volkhov. By the beginning of October, mountains of supplies were piling up there: grain sacks with flour and cereals, barrels and boxes of fats and canned goods, carcasses of meat. The goods were on the ground in the open, stacked in small piles along the shore. The concentration of large quantities of supplies in the immediate vicinity of the enemy caused grave misgivings, since everything could be destroyed by fire. Because water transport was insufficient, however, the amount of goods leaving the port was trifling. Barges and tugs were frequently out of commission through bomb or storm damage.

Although Leningrad's daily consumption of flour alone amounted to 1,100 tons, only 9,800 tons of all kinds of provisions had reached Osinovets over a period of thirty days. In other words, during one month food enough for only eight days had been delivered, and the city had lived through the other twenty-two days on reserves. Such a rate of delivery was both intolerable and dangerous: the calendar read October 12 and the weather forecast was for early freezing. The "dead" period was approaching when the lake would be impassable either by boats or other vehicles.

Thus, on October 13, a group of executives headed by the chairman of the Leningrad Executive Committee, Popkov, left the city by air for Novaya Ladoga and Gostinopolye on instructions of the Military Council. Their mission was to speed-up the "turn-around" of ships and increase food deliveries. The first thing they learned on arrival was that lack of crews and various technical faults were holding some barges out of service. With the assistance of the Ladoga naval command and thanks to the administrative ability of the chief of the trans-shipment base, Major General Shilov, the river barges were repaired and the crews reinforced by experienced sailors of the naval transports. A continuous traffic-control system was now established to supervise the movement of every vessel from Gostinopolye to Ladoga. At the same time, the workers and sailors of the trans-shipment bases, ports, and ships were listening with great attention to what the Leningraders had to say about the situation inside the city. Until then they had heard a great deal about it, but only the fragmentary, sometimes contradictory, accounts of personal experiences as perceived by individual eyewitnesses in their own way. Now they heard the grim truth of the actual situation from officials and learned what was in store for the city and its inhabitants if deliveries of food were not increased.

The accomplishments of the mission increased the amount of food delivered at Osinovets by two and a half times. During the seven-day period, October 14–October 20, five thousand tons of flour reached the port, though actually this rate was trifling too. Moreover, a cold spell had arrived, and the river might now freeze any day near its mouth, where the current was slow and calm, and then water transport must inevitably halt.

At the same time the Germans became active in the area. Gostinopolye's proximity to the front portended nothing but trouble. The risk was too great to permit any delay: all transport—land and river, civilian and military—was mobilized, at the expense of all other supplies and activities, to carry food. Six days and nights of unceasing labor cleared the harbor, and 12,000 tons of flour, 1,500 tons of cereals, and 1,000 tons of meat and fats were moved from Gostinopolye to Novaya Ladoga. The precious cargoes were dispersed along the lake shore near the mouth of the Volkhov River, packed in bales covered with tarpaulin, and carefully camouflaged to match surrounding objects and the local landscape. Subsequent events showed how incalculable a service to the besieged was rendered by this timely transfer of supplies.

On October 23 a series of violent storms began on Lake Ladoga. Dark, raging waves swept over all obstacles in their path and crashed with a roar against the rocky beach. Six heavily loaded barges, caught in the lake by a storm, were tossed from crest to crest like shells and thrown far up the beach. As tribute to the invincible might of the enraged lake, traffic by ship had to be suspended. Transportation resumed on October 27, after three days, and continued until November 15 with interruptions. On that day, sad though it was, transportation of cargo ceased.

The water route of the autumn of 1941 was a great help to the besieged. From September 12 until the cessation of navigation 24,097 tons of grain, flour, and cereals, 1,131 tons of meat and dairy products; and considerable amounts of ammunition, fuel, and other items that were absolutely necessary for the defense of the city were delivered over the lake. Compared with what was needed, the 25,228 tons of food were not very much, but they helped the Leningraders win twenty additional days, and when a fortress is under siege, even one day means a great deal. The labor of the workers, sailors, soldiers, and officers of the river fleet, who gave their sweat and blood (and many, their lives) to defend each ton of grain, meat, and cereals against enemy aircraft, storms, fires, and plunder will not be forgotten.

The distance from Osinovets to Novaya Ladoga, where the small store of provisions lay, was only ninety kilometers by the water route, but after November 15 it was no longer possible to move goods this way. The lake could not be crossed either by sledges or ships. The only transport that could function unhindered by the slush and bad roads of the season was the airplane. The Military Council therefore addressed a request to the government for cargo planes to carry food supplies, and although many major troop units on other fronts were in acute need of transport aircraft at that time, the request of the Leningraders was granted without delay.

On November 16 food supplies from Novaya Ladoga began to be moved by air. The shortness of the distance made it possible to fly five or six round trips a day, and the sound of motors over Lake Ladoga never ceased. The frequency of the flights alerted the Germans, however, and their aircraft began bombing the airfield at Novaya Ladoga. It became dangerous to concentrate any large number of planes there. Thus, two-thirds of the planes were transferred to other, more remote airfields, from which they brought supplies: meat pressed into blocks, lard, smoked foods, canned goods, powdered eggs, condensed milk, butter, and other highly nourishing and compact products.

The meat industry of the USSR, shipping from meat combines throughout the country, greatly aided the besieged in sending them the pressed meat in block form. Unlike carcasses, meat pressed into blocks has the advantage, first of all, of portability. Each block, with sides of equal length and almost square, weighed twenty kilograms and (packed in corrugated wrapping) could load an airplane to capacity. Trans-shipment was easy, and the meat in blocks could be stored for long periods, even if subjected to considerable fluctuations of temperature. Experience with supply during the siege shows the great economic expediency of moving meat this way both to overcome the problems of long distances and the shortage or absence in some regions of refrigeration. One ton of blocked meat stores in a space of 0.65 square meters and ten tons may easily be loaded into a freight car, a space which can accommodate only eight tons of carcass meat. Furthermore, meat in blocks does not soil and thus none need be lost through trimming off soiled parts. Finally, machinery can be used in its loading and unloading.

Following a tight routine, each plane made two flights as a rule from the distant airfields each day: the plane was loaded in no more than twenty minutes and unloaded in ten. The crews became quite exhausted, and their flights often involved battles with German aircraft as well. As protection for each other the cargo planes, armed with machine guns, left the airfields in groups of six or nine. They often had a fighter escort in addition. Since the Fascists feared to attack transport planes when they traveled in groups, such tactics to a large extent insured the safety of a flight.

Sometimes for various technical reasons an airplane would be separated from its group; then enemy fighters would pounce on it. In this way an Li-2, commanded by Zhantiev, was lost with its fine crew. They had averaged three or four round trips a day, delivering food to the city and bringing people out on the return trip. On November 29 Zhantiev was scheduled for a group flight, but for some reason took off four or five minutes after the other aircraft, and these minutes cost him and those with him their lives. When his plane encountered a German fighter over the lake, Zhantiev began to skim the water and his machine gunner opened fire. The fighter was much faster than the cargo plane, however, and gained the upper hand. With sixteen evacuees aboard, Zhantiev's airplane caught fire and vanished into the icy water.

Like hawks, the Messerschmitts lay in wait for solitary aircraft over the lake, but they did not always get away with their bandit behavior. Commanded by the experienced airman Panteli, a lone Li-2 was heading for Leningrad with cargo. A Messerschmitt sighted the solitary plane and attacked. Seeing the danger, Panteli veered sharply to one side, while his gunner fired a burst from his machine gun. The maneuver worked: the pilot of the Messerschmitt was killed or seriously wounded and his machine went out of control, crashing through thin ice to the bottom of Lake Ladoga. Panteli had evened the score for the death of Zhantiev. In those days there were many different cases of tragic deaths. The deadly war went on everywhere.

Hostile aircraft did not stop the air deliveries. Despite great danger the cargo planes daily brought meat, fats, and concentrates to the beleaguered city. Except for these deliveries, the diet of the population would have been very bad indeed. Meat is protein, and protein intake is absolutely necessary for the human organism to restore its tissues and necessary especially in the case of the wounded, the sick, and children. It was for these reasons that meat continued to be delivered to the city despite all difficulties.

Mass transport of food by air under these conditions was a costly procedure: Cargo planes were diverted from use for military purposes; thousands of tons of fuel were expended; and the number of available aircraft was reduced by combat. But while this is true it is also true that the ships of the air saved thousands of human lives, and it was for this noble purpose that they were taken from other fronts and given to Leningrad. The heroic work, the courage, and valor of the airmen will never be forgotten by those who survived the blockade.

At the beginning of November the enemy regrouped his units and launched a new offensive with large forces from the direction of Chudovo toward Volkhov. The Soviet Fourth Army, protecting this important point, could not withstand the attacks and began to retreat. Exploiting this success, the Germans increased their pressure in an effort to take Volkhov in a continuous advance, reach Lake Ladoga, encircle the Fifty-fourth Army defending Leningrad on the southeastern side of the lake, and thereby sever the last line of communication between the city and the rest of the country. What the Fascist commanders regarded as a most alluring prospect looked extremely ominous to the Leningraders. Enemy divisions were pushing Soviet troops back; hostile forward units had entered Gostinopolye and were approaching nearer and nearer to Volkhov. There was a real threat that this important strategic point might be lost. At the urgent request of the Leningrad Front Military Council, Supreme Headquarters placed the commander of the Fifty-fourth Army, Major General (now General of the Army) I. I. Fedyuninsky, in charge of the defense of Volkhov. To his command were now transferred the retreating troops on the right flank of the Fourth Army, and some three thousand men and officers were brought from Leningrad by transport aircraft to reinforce his forward units. Partisan detachments that had been formed for operations against the enemy's rear were also put under his orders.

Fedyuninsky utilized this assistance swiftly and intelligently. He reinforced the retreating units on the right flank of the Fourth Army with the men and officers transferred from Leningrad and strengthened them with weapons and ammunition. In a short time their combat capability was restored. To improve his defenses, Fedyuninsky resorted to extreme measures: the anti-aircraft guns covering Volkhov were moved up to the front lines and used as field artillery and two-thirds of the machine guns of the naval launches were removed and assigned to the army. The regrouping of his units was carried out quickly and went unnoticed by enemy intelligence. Along the whole front resistance to the enemy increased. The Fascist German offensive slowed down and in two days came to a halt. Repeated enemy attempts to smash the hastily organized defense and continue the offensive that had begun so successfully did not materialize.

Many German soldiers left their bones on the approaches to Volkhov. The heavy losses, however, which Hitler's headquarters had ostensibly been "trying to avoid" by canceling the direct assault on Leningrad did not cancel the attack on Volkhov. Army Group North was ordered to forge another ring around the besieged city before the onset of cold weather. After reorganizing his forces, the enemy launched an attack on Voibokalo while simultaneously exerting strong pressure on Volkhov in a move calculated to break through the defense somewhere and reach the lake. The Germans knew that the Soviet defenders were holding this sector of the front by a thin line of hurriedly dug trenches. If it could be pierced at any one point, the road to Lake Ladoga would be open. But the enemy could not break the resistance of the men of the Fifty-fourth Army, despite bold and stubborn attacks. The assault was beaten off, this time for a long while.

It is interesting to note that, having failed in its offensive, the other side could find nothing cleverer than to announce by radio that Fedyuninsky, the commander of the Fifty-fourth Army, had committed suicide in despair over his unsuccessful conduct of operations at Volkhov. Later the German people came to know the sheer falsity of this statement, for in the course of the war Army Commander Fedyuninsky was repeatedly mentioned in dispatches of the Supreme Commander of the Soviet Armed Forces for the excellent performance of the troops entrusted to his command.

As the Fascist troops approached Volkhov, the Leningrad Front Military Council had issued an order that all basic equipment of the Volkhov hydroelectric plant should be dismantled and sent to the interior of the country; in case of a direct threat of capture and at the discretion of the Army Commander, the plant and the dam were to be blown up. In compliance with this order the equipment, except two small auxiliary hydroturbines, was dismantled and sent off, and the plant and dam were prepared for demolition; it only remained to light the fuse and everything would go up. A heavy weight of responsibility rested on Fedyuninsky's shoulders. Duty and military honor would not permit him to blow up the plant before the enemy set foot on the dam. Fighting confidently and selflessly on the nearest approaches to Volkhov, he fulfilled the task assigned to him honorably: the enemy did not take Volkhov or Voibokalo, and the line of communication across Lake Ladoga remained under Soviet control. Moreover, saving the hydroelectric plant made it possible to supply current to beleaguered Leningrad by the end of 1942.

The tempting idea of a double envelopment of Leningrad turned into tragedy for the German High Command. Instead of warm living quarters in Volkhov, the German soldiers had to spend the winter on open, swampy terrain. Over the boundless expanses of the surrounding land, slaughtered warriors of the Fascist Reich lay scattered on frozen ground. Instead of an encircled and paralyzed Soviet Fifty-fourth Army, as the enemy had imagined, he saw and felt the formidable power of the beleaguered city's advance guard.

Thanks to the efforts of Soviet fighting men, the provisions at Novaya Ladoga were safe. Covered with tarpaulin, flour, cereals, meat, and fats lay along the lake shore awaiting the winter road. On the other side of the water, impatiently and in torment, people waited for bread.

7

HUNGER

November–December, 1941

NOVEMBER ARRIVED. Cold, cloudy days and heavy snowfalls replaced the clear, dry days of October. The ground was covered by a thick layer of white that rose in drifts along the streets and boulevards. An icy wind drove powdered snow through the slits of dugouts and shelters, through the broken windows of apartments, hospitals, and stores. Winter came early, snowy, and cold.

The functioning of the city's transportation system deteriorated with each day. Fuel supplies were almost gone, and industry was dying out. Workers and employees, quartered in distant parts of the city, had now to walk several kilometers to work, struggling from one end of the city to the other through deep snow. Exhausted at the close of the working day, they could barely make their way home. There they could throw off their clothes and lie down for a short while to stretch their work-heavy legs. Sleep would come instantly, in spite of the cold, but would constantly be interrupted by cramps of the legs or hands. Rising was hard in the morning. Night did not restore the strength or drive away weariness. The fatigue of great temporary exertion will pass off in a single night's rest; but this was weariness that came from the daily exhausting of physical strength. Soon, however, it would be time for work again. Arm, leg, neck, and heart muscles would have to take up their burdens. The brain worked tensely.

The demands on people's strength increased as their nourishment deteriorated. The constant shortage of food, the cold weather and nervous tension wore the workers down. Jokes and laughter ceased; faces grew preoccupied and stern. People were weaker. They moved slowly, stopping often. Rosy cheeks were like a miracle. People looked at the person with surprise and some suspicion. Few people in November paid any attention to the whistle and burst of shells that had shocked them into alertness only a few days before. The thunder of gunfire was like a distant, aimless, hoarse barking. People were deeply absorbed in their joyless thoughts.

The blockade was now fifty-three days old. The most severe economies in food consumption and the delivery of a small quantity of grain across the lake had only resulted in the following meager amounts being on hand on the first of November: flour for fifteen days; cereals for sixteen days; sugar for thirty days; fats for twenty-two days. There was only a very small quantity of meat. The supply of meat products depended almost wholly on the deliveries by air. Out of the whole city, however—although everyone knew that food was scarce, since the rations were being reduced—the actual situation was known to only seven men. Two specially chosen workers recorded the deliveries of food over the lake and air routes (and later over the Ice Road), and these figures and those for food on hand were restricted to a small inner circle, which made it possible to keep the secret of the beleaguered fortress.

The eve of the twenty-fourth anniversary of the October Revolution arrived.[1] There usually was such a happy fuss and bustle on that evening! Streets and houses would have been ablaze with lights; store windows would delight the eye with their decorations and lavish displays of goods. Fat turkeys, apples, prunes, pastries, thin slices of ham, and a world of other delicacies would lure shoppers. Everywhere, marketing would be going on in lively fashion, as families prepared to spend the holidays with friends. There would have been the noise of happy children ex-

[1] The anniversary of the October Revolution is November 7 on the revised calendar.

cited by the gaiety in the air and the prospect of presents and shows.

In the memorable year of 1941, Leningraders were deprived of pleasure. They had cold, darkness, and the sensation of hunger constantly with them. The sight of the empty shelves in the stores woke a feeling of melancholy in them that was actually painful. The holiday was observed by issuing each child two hundred grams of sour cream and one hundred grams of potato flour. Adults received five salted tomatoes. Nothing more was to be found.

The enemy presented his gift to the city of the revolution on the night of November 6. Heavy bombers broke through at great height and dropped explosives at random. The bombs weighed at least one ton each. Falling with a terrifying whistle, some of them destroyed buildings, but many burst at the bottom of the Neva, jarring the majestic structures along the embankments; still others went deep into the ground without exploding.

On the same night the Germans dropped a number of magnetic naval mines attached to large parachutes (up to eighty square meters in area) over the city. These mines were heavier and more destructive than anything previously dropped on the city and one of them fell at the Yegorov plant to constitute a fearful threat to an enterprise that had very great importance to the besieged. The mine had to be disarmed immediately. How was it to be done? The personnel of the local anti-aircraft defense by this time knew how to combat delayed-action bombs of various kinds but knew nothing about disarming naval mines three meters wide. If the bomb were approached with screwdrivers and wrenches of steel, its magnetic relays might be activated. Later it was learned that such a mine must not be jostled while being dismantled, because the detonator and its timing mechanism had a short-duration fuse setting and might have gone off at any moment.

When a captain of engineers, A. F. Litvinov, arrived at the spot, he came with no practical experience in working with these monsters. Improvising, Litvinov first lifted out the small timing mechanism (the so-called inertia detonator); next he removed the large timing mechanism and the impact detonator in that order. The tremendously demanding and complicated operation ended happily. General success in disarming these mines, however, was far from the case, though the Yegorov plant was saved. Many soldiers died in sudden, powerful explosions of the enemy's treacherous new weapon.

Major devastation, however, was avoided. The threat to factories posed by the mines was eliminated, thanks to the selflessness of such noble sons as Litvinov, A. N. Khanukaev, N. M. Lopatin, P. V. Maslov, A. V. Orlovsky, Ya. P. Urbanovich, and many others. It is impossible to mention in these pages all the names of the courageous people who went with their eyes open, conquering fear, to face death in the name of the sacred cause. Their heroic deeds are not forgotten, nonetheless; thousands owe their lives and their homes to them.

A standard technique for disarming magnetic mines was soon worked out in detail on the basis of the experience that had been gained, and many civil defense workers were trained in it. The general morale got a great lift from the successful struggle with the mines.

More serious consequences followed from other events that occurred on the second day of the twenty-fourth anniversary. On November 8, motorized units of the enemy took Tikhvin, a town eighty kilometers east of Volkhov. Relying on the mobility of his troops but exposing his flanks and the overextended line of communications of his units at the same time, Schmidt, the commander of the Thirty-ninth Motorized Corps, drove a wedge deep into our defenses with a quick encircling movement. From the distance between the corps and the main German forces, it may safely be assumed that the capture of Tikhvin on November 8 was dictated more by political considerations than military readiness to carry out the operation and consolidate the results.

It is well known that the Nazi army had tried and failed to capture Leningrad in September. Hitler had then proclaimed his new plan to take the city by hunger. Hunger would be his best ally in annihilating the population. Hitler's propaganda machine, seizing upon this last means of recouping the prestige of the army, had loudly and insistently played up the idea to the German people and to "true believers" outside Germany.

Days, then weeks, passed, but the city did not surrender. Hitler's headquarters categorically demanded that Army Group North push farther east to sever the one remaining route connecting the besieged with the rest of the country. When Schmidt succeeded in throwing back the defenders and taking the important rail station of Tikhvin, German newspapers, radio, and official bulletins began immediately to exaggerate the victory. "Leningrad will now be compelled to surrender without the blood of German soldiers being shed," declared the German press. On November 9 the Berlin radio broadcast every thirty minutes the announcement by the High Command of the German capture of Tikhvin. A brass band played a grand march before each broadcast. People's expectations were aroused by the unusually theatrical way in which late developments were presented. A wrought-up public opinion in Germany and other countries awaited the supreme event: the imminent fall of the Bolshevik stronghold.

For whatever reason of military or political calculation, the Germans had struck at a very sensitive spot. The loss of Tikhvin brought much hardship to the defenders, particularly in supplying troops and population with food, fuel, and ammunition. Rumor of its fall sped through the city from person to person as though carried on the wind, even before a Soviet communiqué announced the enemy's seizure of small, isolated Tikhvin, lost somewhere in the forests of Leningrad *oblast*. There was alarm and confusion among the besieged. By what routes could supplies now be brought in? How long could present supplies last? There were good grounds for uneasiness. Only a very little grain was left, and supply trains from the interior of Russia would now have to halt at the small station of Zaborye, 160 kilometers by horse over country and forest roads from Volkhov. To make possible the transport of supplies by truck from the station at Zaborye to Osinovets, it would be necessary to build a road more than two hundred kilometers long through thick woodland. To avoid Tikhvin, the route between Zaborye and Osinovets would have to be more than 320 kilometers over-all. Moreover, though a truck road of such length would require much time and great effort to build, there were grave apprehensions that at capacity it would still fail to supply the population and troops with enough food to meet even the lowest hunger ration.

Despite these sobering calculations of the slightness of the advantage to be gained and the prospect that passage over the road would be rough and painful, the road was as necessary to the defenders as oxygen. Soon after the loss of Tikhvin, then, the Military Council ordered the building of an automobile road over the following general route: Osinovets–Lednevo–Novaya Ladoga–Karpino–Yamskoe–Novinka–Yeremina Gora–Shugozero–Nikulskoe–Lakhta–Veliki Dvor–Serebryanskaya–Zaborye. The plan would take into account the need for a goods turnover at both ends of two thousands tons a day, with a front-line trans-shipment base to be placed at Zaborye. (See Map 5.) The actual construction

TABLE 17

Flour............for 24 days, of which 17 days' supply was at Novaya Ladoga
Cereals..........for 18 days, of which 10 days' supply was at Novaya Ladoga
Fats.............for 17 days, of which 3 days' supply was at Novaya Ladoga
Meat products.....for 9 days, of which 9 days' supply was at Novaya Ladoga
Sugar............for 22 days

was assigned to military units of the Rear Services and to collective farmers of adjacent settlements.

The decision aroused some hopes, however feeble, that food and other indispensable goods would arrive when the road was finished. A time limit of fifteen days was set for construction. The food reserves in Leningrad and Novaya Ladoga on November 9 are given in Table 17 (in day's supplies).

In addition to these supplies, air transport brought in small quantities of meat, fats, and other very nourishing foods.

Although very little food was left, it would have been possible to manage until the opening of the new road without lowering civilian or military rations, except that two-thirds of the flour and more than half of the grain were on the other side of the lake, and the lake was now beginning to freeze where it was shallow, with only vessels of the naval flotilla able to get through, with difficulty. The ships carried ammunition, which was sorely needed,

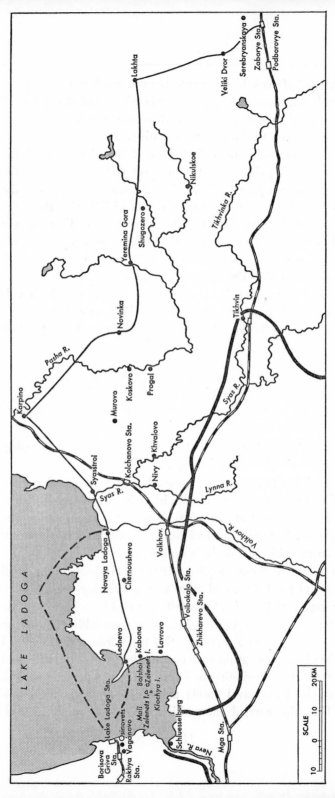

MAP 5.—Supplying Leningrad after the fall of Tikhvin

and some food, Although the weather forecast now called for lower temperatures in five or six days, it was impossible to predict when traffic would move over the ice. The situation required an immediate cutback in food consumption, and the Military Council ordered a reduction in bread and meat rations for all personnel of the army and the Baltic Fleet while maintaining civilian rations at their current level.

In coming to this decision, the Military Council had reasoned as follows:

a) The rations of the residents of the city were already scanty; further reduction was virtually impossible.

b) The reduction in rations would have less effect on the physical condition of front-line soldiers and sailors, who were then receiving eight hundred grams of bread daily, or of soldiers of the rear units, who were receiving six hundred grams of bread daily and some good hot food.

TABLE 18

	Bread	Meat
Front-line Troops...	600	125
Rear Units........	400	50

c) The saving thus achieved by reducing the ration of the military would make possible the stretching of grain reserves through the time until the Winter Road would be ready.

So they thought, calculated, and hoped.

An order to the troops on November 8 introduced the new ration levels for bread and meat. They are listed (in grams per day) in Table 18.

Fresh fish had disappeared completely from the food ration. There was none, nor was there any possibility of replacing it with something else. Canned fish and crabmeat could be substituted for an equal weight of meat; potatoes and vegetables could be exchanged for cereals, at the rate of ten grams of cereals for one hundred grams of vegetables.

Army military councils, commanders and commissars of large formations, units, and installations were ordered to establish very strict control over food consumption: rations were not to be increased in the rear and second echelons at the expense of front-line troops. Violators would be brought to trial.

Five days passed. The air temperature sank to six or seven degrees, but the waters of Lake Ladoga did not freeze and a winter road over the lake could not be built. No one could grant the Leningraders' passionate wish for a reliable layer of ice to form over the lake. The hopes and calculations of the Military Council had collapsed. Bread was running out. Time had begun to work against the besieged. Hard and painful though it was, the civilian bread ration, too, had to be cut once more. Beginning November 13, factory workers were to receive three hundred grams of bread a day, while office workers, dependents, and children under twelve would receive 150 grams. The personnel who ate in messes—militarized security units, fire brigades, fighter detachments, members of vocational and industrial-technical schools—were to receive three hundred grams.

These measures made possible the reduction of the total daily expenditure of flour to 622 tons, a level which itself could only be maintained for a few days. On the lake it was storming. High winds drove waves against the shore and cracked the brittle ice that had formed. Such weather made certain that provisions from Novaya Ladoga would not arrive soon. Supplies within the city were nearly exhausted.

In order to avoid having to cut off the distribution of bread completely at any time (and thereby paralyze the city), the Military Council lowered rations for the third time in November only seven days after the reduction of November 13. From November 20 on, workers were to receive 250 grams of bread a day; office workers, dependents, and children, 125 grams; front-line troops, naval crews, and flying and ground personnel of the air force, 500 grams; all other military units would receive 300 grams.[2] The

---

[2] In a book of articles entitled *The City of Great Lenin* (Leningrad Publishing House, 1957), p. 110, it is stated that from November 20 on front-line troops and commanders received 300 grams of bread a day, all others 150 grams. This is an obvious mistake. The author of the article, F. E. Sirota, has not taken into account the fact that in addition to bread, from November 20 through December 11, 1941, in compliance with a directive from the Leningrad Front Military Council on November 19, 1941,

daily outlay of flour (including admixtures) was now at the lowest point of the entire blockade, 510 tons. Not more than thirty carloads of flour per day were used to feed a population of two and one-half million people. To procure even this much required hard fighting with the enemy and the elements.

The sudden drop by more than one-third in the bread ration had pernicious effects on health. Everyone, dependents especially, began to experience acute hunger. Men and women faded before each others' eyes; they moved slowly, they talked slowly; then an emaciated body would suddenly be lifeless. In those days, death drew itself up to its full stature and loomed menacingly, preparing to reap in masses those who crossed its path, regardless of sex or age.

The trials endured were incredible; they were far worse than anything experienced either during the First World War or the immediate post–Civil War period, itself a time of ruin and hardship. Yet the moral fortitude of the population remained unshaken. Even now, after almost twenty years, it is difficult to understand how people endured such prolonged acute hunger. But the truth is indisputable; the Leningraders found strength within themselves to stand their ground and hold their city.

Although the number of inhabitants remained approximately unchanged, the daily expenditure of flour had been reduced by more than 400 per cent during the 107 days of blockade up to December 25. The distribution of flour per day by periods is given in Table 19 (in tons).[3]

Like pictures, numbers are perceived and interpreted in different ways. Sometimes a cursory glance is enough; more often it takes time to comprehend them fully and deeply. The figures

there was also a daily issue of hardtack: 100 grams for front-line troops and 75 grams for others, which corresponded to 200 and 150 grams of bread. Beginning December 12, the issue of hardtack was discontinued and the troops began again to receive only bread: 500 and 300 grams, respectively.

[3] The figures on expenditure of flour during the indicated periods are taken from the decisions of the Leningrad Front Military Council during 1941.

below show the extreme irregularity of flour consumption from period to period and suggest that the reduction on November 20 might have been avoided.

The extremely limited supply of flour required daily consumption to be reduced from 622 tons to 510 tons on November 20. On that date the bread ration was reduced for both the civil and military population, bringing it to 125 grams per day for most people, while the drop in total outlay amounted to 112 tons a day. Consumption of flour had thus been reduced by a total of 3,808 tons in a period of thirty-four days from November 20 to Decem-

TABLE 19

Beginning of Blockade–September 11	2,100
September 11–September 16	1,300
September 16–October 1	1,100
October 1–October 26	1,000
October 26–November 1	880
November 1–November 13	735
November 13–November 20	622
November 20–December 25	510

TABLE 20

DAILY CONSUMPTION (In Tons)*

	September	October	November	December
Meat and Meat products...	146	119	92	80
Cereals, Macaroni.........	220	220	140	115
Sugar, Confectionery.......	202	142	140	104

* Not including the Leningrad Front and the Baltic Fleet.

ber 25. The figures also show, however, that the same amount of flour could have been saved in five days in September had the first cut been made on September 5 rather than September 11. The step was not taken for reasons already given. One must also take into account, naturally, the difficulties of prediction and calculation when the enemy was at the gates. It was hardly clear in September what a five-day saving of provisions might mean for the population in November.

Although the reduced ration levels introduced in September for meat and cereals, and in November for sugar and confectionery, were not changed until 1942, daily consumption of these foods steadily decreased, as shown by Table 20.

The decrease was achieved by limiting the distribution of food

Fig. 8.—The caption on the poster reads: "Death to the Child Killers!" (Courtesy of Sovfoto.)

Fig. 9.—Leningrad citizens clearing the streets of snow and ice. (Courtesy of Sovfoto.)

Fig. 8.—The caption on the poster reads: "Death to the Child Killers!" (Courtesy of Sovfoto.)

Fig. 9.—Leningrad citizens clearing the streets of snow and ice. (Courtesy of Sovfoto.)

Fig. 10.—In the summer of 1942, cases of American food appeared at the food bases on Lake Ladoga. They were addressed to Moscow but had been rerouted. (Courtesy of Sovfoto.)

FIG. 11.—In the spring, fountains spurted from under the wheels of the trucks as they moved over the flooded road. But until the steamers could sail the lake again, the trucks continued to carry food to the city. (Courtesy of Sovfoto.)

Fɪɢ. 12.—A terminus of one of the tracks across the lake. The sign reads: "Lenfront Ice Road. Distance thirty kilometers." (Courtesy of Sovfoto.)

FIG. 13.—A victim of the starvation is carried to the cemetery. (Courtesy of Sovfoto.)

Fig. 14.—Bodies were taken to the edge of the city by relatives or friends, who were too weak to dig the grave. Special squads were given extra rations to bury the dead. (Courtesy of Sovfoto.)

Fig. 15.—Houses along the streets were boarded up for protection against explosions. One of the posters shown advertises an entertainment. (Courtesy of Sovfoto.)

in dining rooms and cafeterias to the amounts due on ration cards. If in September, for example, fifty tons of a total expenditure of 146 tons of meat were allotted to the dining rooms—thus giving the workers served by them so much food over and above the stipulated ration—only ten tons were distributed this way in December and only to the cafeterias of the most important defense plants. The situation was similar with other foods. In effect there was now introduced (with few exceptions) a 100-per-cent accounting for all foods served in the dining rooms. Whether people ate in dining rooms or at home, their food in December consisted exclusively of what they could obtain by means of their ration cards. Indeed, the only food actually distributed every day to the inhabitants was bread. Other supplies were passed out once in ten days, and not always then. Assuming for the moment, however, that factory and office workers did receive their rations in full and spread them evenly over the thirty-day periods, the daily food situation would have been as given in Table 21.

Obviously, the caloric values given here are questionable. As mentioned above, meat was rarely issued in December; and other products—powdered eggs, canned goods, sheepgut jelly, vegetable-blood sausage—were usually substituted for it. There were also days when the population received no meat or fats at all. For cereals the issue was chiefly made up of pearl barley, oatmeal, and split peas. Macaroni was often given instead of rye flour. Even using the overstated estimate, however, it is obvious that an adult's normal daily need for 3,000–3,500 calories was, so to speak, "forgotten." More than half the food volume of this hunger ration was simply bread: consumption of protein, fats, vitamins, and mineral salts became catastrophically small. So hard and torturous a time had arrived that it is difficult for anyone who did not live through it to know what it was like.

To fill their empty stomachs and deaden the pains of a hunger which can be compared to nothing else, the inhabitants resorted to all sorts of ways to procure food. They trapped crows and hunted down the surviving dogs and cats. They took anything that could be used as food from their medicine chests: castor oil, Vaseline, glycerin. Soup and jelly were prepared from carpenter's glue. But by no means all the people of the vast city had these supplementary sources of nourishment available to them.

Life was especially hard for children who had just turned twelve. At twelve a "dependent's" ration card replaced the "child's" card which had been good until then. His food ration was cut just as the child was growing adult enough to take active part in the work of disarming incendiary bombs and to bear on

TABLE 21

Factory Workers and Eingineer-Technical Workers

Bread	250 grams
Fats	20 grams
Meat	50 grams
Cereals	50 grams
Sugar and Confectionery	50 grains
Total	420 grams (1,087 calories)

Office Workers

Bread	125 grams
Fats	8.3 grams
Meat	26.6 grams
Sugar and Confectionery	33.3 grams
Cereals	33.3 grams
Total	226.5 grams (581 calories)

Dependents

Bread	125 grams
Fats	6.6 grams
Meat	13.2 grams
Sugar and Confectionery	26.6 grams
Cereals	20.0 grams
Total	191.4 grams (466 calories)

Children under 12

Bread	125 grams
Fats	16.6 grams
Meat	13.2 grams
Sugar and Confectionery	40.0 grams
Cereals	40.0 grams
Total	234.8 grams (684 calories)

his weak shoulders some of the heavy work and responsibility of his home. Parents sometimes denied themselves bread to support the enfeebled bodies of their children but in the process did severe harm to their own bodies.

Cold had settled down to stay in the unheated apartments of the city. Remorselessly it froze the exhausted people. Dystrophy and cold sent 11,085 people to their graves during November, the first to fall under death's scythe being the old men. Their bodies, in contrast to those of women of the same age or young men, offered no resistance at all to acute hunger.

The health services set up a widespread network of medical stations to help people survive. Various treatments were tried: injections of cardiovascular preparations, intravenous glucose injections, a little hot wine. These measures saved many lives, but the "forgotten" minimum human food requirement continued to make itself felt. More and more adults and children died every day. First a person's arms and legs grew weak, then his body became numb, the numbness gradually approached the heart, gripped it as in a vise, and then the end came.

Death overtook people anywhere. As he walked along the street, a man might fall and not get up. People would go to bed at home and not rise again. Often death would come suddenly as men worked at their machines.

Since public transportation was not operating, burial was a special problem. The dead were usually carried on sleds without coffins. Two or three relatives or close friends would haul the sled along the seemingly endless streets, often losing strength and abandoning the deceased halfway to the cemetery, leaving to the authorities the task of disposing of the body. Employees of the municipal public services and health service cruised the streets and alleys to pick up the bodies, loading them on trucks. Frozen bodies, drifted over with snow, lined the cemeteries and their approaches. There was not strength enough to dig into the deeply frozen earth. Civil defense crews would blast the ground to make mass graves, into which they would lay tens and sometimes hundreds of bodies without even knowing the names of those they buried.

—May the dead forgive the living who could not, under those desperate conditions, perform the last ceremonies due honest, laborious lives.

Exceeding the previous month's mortality by almost five times, 52,881 people died of dystrophy in December and still more people of various ages reached the threshold of death. In January and February the death rate reached its peak. During these sixty days 199,187 persons died. At every step furious death tore from the besieged their battle comrades, friends, and relatives. Although the pain of loss was sharp and piercing, the great wave of death did not spread despair among the survivors. The Leningraders died like heroes, striking at the enemy till their last breath. Their deaths summoned the living to an even more dedicated struggle, which went on with unprecedented stubbornness.

It is of scientific interest that Leningrad was free of epidemics during this period, and that the incidence of acute and infectious disease was less in December, 1941, than in the same month in 1940. Details of the comparison are given in Table 22.

TABLE 22

NUMBER OF CASES OF DISEASE*

	December 1940	December 1941
Typhoid Fever	143	114
Dysentery	2,086	1,778
Typhus	118	42
Scarlet Fever	1,056	93
Diphtheria	728	211
Whooping Cough	1,844	818

* From a report of the Leningrad Health Service, January 5, 1942.

How is the absence of epidemics to be explained, given conditions of acute hunger, shortage of hot water, lack of protection from cold weather, and physical weakness? Leningrad's experience proves that hunger need not be accompanied by the inseparable fellow travelers, infectious disease and epidemics. A good system of sanitation breaks up their comradeship, for not only during the winter months of 1941 but in the spring of 1942, when conditions were most favorable for outbreaks of disease, no epidemics occurred in Leningrad. The government set the people to cleaning streets, yards, staircases, garrets, cellars, sewer wells—in brief, all the breeding grounds where infectious disease might start. From the end of March to the middle of April, 300,000 persons worked daily at cleaning up the city. Inspections of living quarters and compulsory observance of rules for cleanliness prevented the spread of communicable disease. The inhabitants were starving. Nonetheless, they fulfilled to their last days the social obligations necessary in a crowded community.

Hunger left a heavy mark on the people: the body was wasted, slow, and dull. But microbes apparently did not grow in such bodies. Parchment-thin skin and bones evidently failed to provide the necessary environment for infectious germs. Perhaps this is not the explanation of the relative absence of disease; some other force, not understood by science as yet, may have been operating, for there are still so many secrets in nature. It is also possible that some unfavorable factors may have canceled others. Whatever the reason, however, it is a fact that there were no epidemics and, in fact, the number of cases of infectious disease decreased just at the time that alimentary dystrophy was at its height. There was one outbreak of scurvy in the spring of 1942 as a result of the prolonged malnutration, but scurvy was soon banished from Leningrad with very few fatalities.

The great death rate of December and the early months of 1942 was the result of the prolonged and acute shortage of food brought on by the blockade.

During the period of the blockade, 632,000 people died of starvation. Their deaths are mourned by all Soviet citizens. The painful figure is given here to suggest the depth of suffering endured in Leningrad.

Cities had been blockaded before in human history, and men had fought and suffered and perished. But in general the laws of war had somehow been observed. In the Second World War, Hitler tossed all international agreements onto the trash pile, trampled on moral standards of behavior in wartime, and unleashed the animal instincts of the German soldiers. On June 14, 1941, just before his attack on the USSR, he declared at a meeting of his commanders that it would be necessary to employ more brutal methods against the Soviet Union than against the Western countries. Keitel testified to this at the Nuremberg trials: "Hitler mainly stressed that this was a decisive battle between two ideologies and that this fact excluded the possibility of employing in the war [with Russia] the methods familiar to us soldiers and which according to international law were the only ones considered proper."[4]

Despite their monstrousness, Hitler's instructions were carried out to the letter by his commanders. They approved the dictator's policy of annihilating our people. The Fascist troops laid waste our spacious countryside and our cities with violence and wrath, and they killed without regarding age or sex. They threw themselves on Leningrad with frenzy and malignant joy. Leningrad, one of the most important political and economic centers of the country, was especially hated. The Fascists wanted to destroy the population of the city physically, before the eyes of the whole world. "From our point of view, in this war that is a life-and-death struggle, there is no profit in preserving even a part of the population of this large city," are the words of a directive from the chief of the German Naval Operations Staff attached to Army Group North.[5] Only through the Leningraders' inflexible will to victory, their burning hatred of the invaders, and the firm leadership of Front, party, and Soviet agencies did the spirit of the population remain adamant in the face of this terror. The energetic action of the Soviet government in delivering food, war matériel, and other necessary supplies, as well as by diversionary military strokes, frustrated the base designs of the Fascists.

German doctors informed the world in 1947 that the population of the western zone of Germany was starving to death. The population was then receiving a ration of eight hundred calories per person per day. The doctors accused the victorious countries of deliberately destroying the German people by starvation. They wrote in their memorandum:

> We consider it our duty as German doctors to declare to the entire world that what is taking place here is the direct opposite of the "education in the spirit of democracy" which we were promised; it is, on the contrary, the destruction of the biological basis of democracy. The spiritual and physical destruction of a great nation is taking place before our eyes,

[4] Nuremberg Trial Stenographic Account.

[5] Berlin, September 29, 1941, No. 1-1a 1601/41 ("Future of the City of Petersburg"). Translation from German.

and no one can escape responsibility for this unless he does everything in his power to rescue and help.[6]

In reality, as De Castro correctly points out, the allies had no intention of starving the population of Germany: "the low ration levels in the postwar period in Germany were the natural consequence of the destructive war and the disintegration of the world's economy which it produced."[7] It was the fault of the Germans, in other words, that hunger gripped a number of countries including Germany itself.

German doctors found powerful words and means to appeal to the consciences of the peoples of the world against "the destruction of a great nation" when hunger reached Germany and the German people began to feel privation, although this was nothing compared to the tortures the Leningraders endured. The same doctors had uttered not a word of protest against the undisguised efforts of their compatriots, the officials of Fascist Germany, to destroy the peaceful population of Leningrad by starvation.

Order was maintained strictly in Leningrad. It was supported by the authorities and by the people themselves under conditions when the incessant gnawing of hunger might have been expected to drive them to break the law. For example, a truck driver was hurrying to deliver fresh bread in time for the opening of the stores. At the corner of Rastannaya and Ligovka streets a shell burst near the truck. The front part of the body was sheared off as by a scythe, and loaves of bread spilled out over the pavement. The driver had been killed by a shell splinter; all around it was still dark. The situation could hardly have been better for theft. Yet, having seen the unguarded bread, passers-by turned in the alarm, surrounded the spot, and did not leave until a second truck arrived with the delivery manager of the bread plant. The loaves were collected and delivered to the stores. The hungry people guarding the wrecked truck had, of course, felt the urge to eat;

[6] Josué de Castro, *Geography of Hunger*, p. 328.

[7] *Ibid.*, p. 329.

the aroma of the still warm bread had inflamed their desire for food. The temptation was truly great, but their sense of duty overcame it.

. . . One evening a thickset man entered a bread store on one of the quiet streets in Volodarsky *raion*. After carefully and distrustfully inspecting the customers and the two saleswomen in the store, he suddenly jumped over the counter to the bread and began to throw loaves from the shelves to the customers. He shouted: "Take the loaves! They want to starve us, stand your ground, demand bread!" When the stranger noticed that no one was taking the bread or giving him any support, he struck a saleswoman and made for the door, but all the customers threw themselves on the provocateur and held him for the authorities.

Tens of thousands of letters from citizens were sent to the City Party Committee and the Leningrad City Executive Committee during the blockade. They came from workers, office workers, scholars, housewives—from people in every category of life. Not one expressed despair or spite. Not one revealed an opinion that differed markedly from the general mood of the city. The letters expressed concern for strengthening the defenses of Leningrad. They contained proposals for more rational utilization of materials in production of war supplies and for the preservation of unique equipment, buildings, and monuments. Simple people shared their thoughts, advising how to bear adversity and preserve the city.

There are hundreds of other examples of the remarkable behaviour and highmindedness of the citizens of this large city. Although firewood was not obtainable and people suffered unspeakably from the cold, the trees in the parks and gardens were jealously protected. Leningrad's example under siege and starvation refutes the arguments of the foreign writers who assert that man loses his morals and becomes a predatory beast when hunger affects him powerfully. If this were true, anarchy should have reigned in Leningrad, where two and one-half millions went hungry for a very long time.

Here it will be appropriate to tell a story which reveals dramatically how it was with the besieged during the worst days of the starvation.

There is in Leningrad an Institute of Plant Genetics whose personnel had at one time assembled a rare collection of grain cultures from 118 countries of the world. The work had been done under the direction of Nikolai Ivanovich Vavilov, the famous scientist.[8] By the beginning of the war, the collection contained more than 100,000 different samples of wheat, rye, corn, rice, and other cereal and bean cultures. A broad study of these flora from all over the world had helped agricultural workers in our country solve a number of important problems.

The war interrupted the creative work of the Institute. Many of its people went to the front, where a number died. The Institute of Plant Genetics (and not only it) dropped from sight in the commotion of the war. The authorities had no time for it, as the workers of the Institute knew; they understood they could do as they pleased with the collection, and no one would hold them responsible if the seed samples disappeared. The members of the Institute, despite the loss of colleagues from their ranks, continued to work, adjusting to circumstances as they arose.

When the enemy was approaching the city, the Institute prepared to evacuate the collection. After having been packed and loaded onto freight cars, the seeds and other scientifically valuable objects finally could not be shipped off because of the blockade. The director of the Institute, I. G. Eichfeld, took steps then to store the samples at the Institute on shelves specially equipped to preserve the seeds. A twenty-four hour watch was kept on them. Every Institute employee took a hand in the watch without exception. They disarmed dozens of incendiary bombs that fell on the roof of the building.

Rats caused a great deal of trouble. The creatures easily got into the empty rooms where the collection was stored, climbed up to the shelves, gnawed through packing, and devoured the seeds.

[8] Vavilov (1887–1943?) was Russia's leading plant geneticist and at one time head of the Academy of Agricultural Sciences. He was ousted in 1940 for opposing the theories of T. D. Lysenko and imprisoned. He was "rehabilitated" posthumously.

To protect the collection against the invasion of rats, the seeds were repacked in rat-proof metal boxes and stacked in piles so that they could be under the constant surveillance of the scientists. During the first two months of the blockade, the struggle was chiefly with bombs, rats, and isolated sallies by marauders. More strenuous ordeals were in store for the workers during the famine of November and December, 1941, and the beginning of 1942. This enemy dealt them fearful blows.

In December, Institute employees were often too exhausted to get out of bed, and their work fell to those who could still move about. On one of the coldest days of that dreadful month, the workers heard sorrowful news; their comrade A. Ya. Molibog, the agrometeorologist, had been burned to death in a fire at his home. He had grown so weak from hunger that he could not leave his apartment when it was enveloped in flames. Not long after, the biologist S. A. Egis and D. S. Ivanov, the senior scientist in rice culture, died of exhaustion. Twenty-eight other employees of the Institute followed them to the grave from the same cause.

These people all remained interested in the collection to the end. They would smile and their cloudy eyes would brighten when they were told it was still under care and safe. They had devoted their lives to science, and the consciousness that they had performed their final duties honorably gave them a radiant, joyous feeling, and with this feeling they entered eternity. A small group of scientists now remained alive: K. A. Panteleeva, V. F. Antropova, A. I. Mordvinkina, O. A. Voskresenskaya, R. Ya. Kordon, N. R. Ivanov, V. S. Lekhnovich, M. M. Yakubtsiner, T. I. Mikheeva, P. N. Petrova, and K. T. Chernyavskaya. Headed by Director Eichfeld, they continued with the project of saving the collection at any cost. Hardly able to move their feet, they came to the Institute everyday to work. The fate of the collection depended on their self-control. The proximity to grain and the duty of caring for it in the name of the future while slowly dying of starvation was inhuman torture. But by their solidarity and single-mindedness, the Vavilov collection, which took years to put together, was preserved for science and the future. It cost the lives of many people wholeheartedly devoted to the cause of science, but they triumphed over their suffering.[9]

The people of Leningrad behaved stoically and proudly during the blockade. They preserved the wholeness of the human personality to the last minute of their lives under conditions of incredible privation and acute hunger. There is an inherent feeling among Soviet people that is stronger than death. It is love for the society they have created, and this feeling guided their struggles with the invaders, hunger, and other deprivations.

Life in the beleaguered city took its course.

The front-line soldiers continued to wear the enemy down with active operations. In the process, they sustained large losses, and the wounded crowded the hospitals, where conditions deteriorated as time went on. The wards were now half-dark; plywood and cardboard replaced window glass broken by explosions. Electricity was now irregular owing to the fuel shortage, and the water system did not work. Bombardments and cold spells created incredible difficulties. Even under these conditions, medical results were often brilliant. By devoted care, immediate attention, and quick surgical intervention, lives were saved that were within an inch of death. Most of the wounded went back to the front after recovery, where their experience was very much needed to help the younger soldiers conserve their strength while fighting to win. To speed the recovery of the wounded and sick, the Military Council ordered the issuance of the following daily supplement to their basic rations: twenty grams of powdered eggs, five grams of powdered cocoa, and two grams of dried mushrooms. The wounded were to be given first priority on everything that was available.

Shortage of blood for transfusions hampered recoveries and sometimes caused deaths. Although there were many volunteer

[9] Soon after the end of the war, an article by Darlington was published in the London magazine *Nature* in which the author reported that the noted world collection of seeds assembled by the All-Union Institute of Plant Genetics had been eaten up by hungry people during the blockade of Leningrad.

The reader himself can grade the author of this fabrication.

donors, people had been too weakened by their hunger ration to give blood without serious injury to their own health. "It is absolutely necessary to help out the donors with food and to have blood for wounded soldiers," said Zhdanov. With this in mind, a special ration scale was established on December 9 for blood donors. To the usual daily ration were added two hundred grams of bread, thirty grams of fats, forty grams of meat, twenty-five grams of sugar, thirty grams of confectionery, thirty grams of cereals, twenty-five grams of canned fish, and half an egg. The ration enabled donors to give blood twice in three months without injury to their health.

The scholars who had stayed on in the city, refusing at first to be evacuated, had to endure the same privations as anyone else in the dark period of blockade. Many of them, especially the elderly, were dying of starvation. When Zhdanov learned this, he had a list of the scholars prepared, looked it over, and dispatched it to the municipal departments of trade, with instructions to issue enough supplementary rations to maintain them in health. This minimal outlay of food saved the lives of many.

Lumberjacks and workers in the peat bogs received 375 grams of bread a day, which was 125 grams more than the standard worker's ration. Drawn chiefly from the ranks of the Comsomol, the lumberjacks gave their last ounce of strength to keep the key enterprises (e.g., bread factories and dining rooms) in operation and to provide a little heat for the civilian and military hospitals. They worked in bitter cold up to the waist in snow and needed a much bigger and better ration than they received.

The lack of fuel resulted in the freezing of the water pipes—and of people. Firewood is necessary to heat water and since there was none, furniture, books, fences, and houses were burned instead. A great many houses were dismantled and burned to warm the living quarters and the dormitories in the suburb of Okhta. It all burned too fast, like fireworks.

When life is normal and there is fuel, it would appear that only a bit of wood is needed to heat water and prepare a meal, two or three sticks perhaps. The city dweller never realizes what a quantity of fuel a city like Leningrad takes as a whole. To run the city's economy more or less normally, one hundred and twenty train-loads of wood a day are required. They were now throwing in only three or four trainloads of wood in a day; both the supply of wood and peat and the carrying capacity of the railroads were in-adequate. No amount of houses and barns, fences and furniture would make up for the missing firewood. Houses were without light, water, or heat. Like pieces of sculpture, they watched the human drama; the suffering of the people and their desire to live. If people did manage to fetch water home with great difficulty and to carry it safely up the ice-covered steps of the steep stair-cases, heating it was a problem that could not be solved. In December the City Executive Committee opened public centers at dining rooms, large apartment houses, and on the streets to sup-ply boiling water. The measure brought great joy and relief to the population.

Time went on. Everyone, children and adults alike, strove to master hunger. They lived and worked in the firm hope that right would triumph. They did not murmur against fate; each one felt a modest pride that he, along with the rest, was fighting in this diffi-cult time for his beloved city and the honor of the motherland. Despite the hardships and no matter how long the road might be, the engineer, the smith, the scientist, and the woodcutter were roused to heroism by the holy feeling of a just cause. This feeling inspired the artists, too, when they sang and played to divert other hungry, tired people, although their own legs were giving way and they could hardly speak for hoarseness. Only real patriots and people strong in heart could have endured such hardships.

Almost all the theatrical companies were evacuated to the in-terior in good time. The operetta company, however, remained, and the population loved them. As they listened to the jokes, the witty remarks, and the music, the audience escaped for a few hours the constant burden of their thoughts.

A fantastic picture rises before the eyes. December. Twenty-five degrees of frost outside. It would be a little warmer in the un-heated theater, but the room would be full of people in street clothing with many of the older people wearing their felt boots. At three o'clock in the afternoon the operetta *Rose Marie* began.

The artists wore only light costumes; their faces were pinched and pale, but smiling. The ballerinas were so thin it seemed they must break in two if they moved. Between acts many performers would faint, but human will power conquered tired flesh. They would get up, fall, rise again, and continue to perform though they could hardly see.

It was a rare performance that went off without a hitch. In the midst of the play the sound of sirens would pierce the air to warn of danger. When this happened, an intermission would be announced and the audience was led from the theater to an air-raid shelter. At the same time the performers would clamber up to the icy roof to stand guard in the tower in their grease paint and costumes. They were armed with tongs for dislodging incendiary bombs. After the all clear, the hall would fill with the spectators again and the actors, down from the roof, would continue the play. At the end of each performance the public rose. Too weak to applaud, they signified their gratitude by standing silently and reverently for several minutes. The Leningraders appreciated the performers. They understood at what a price and by what a maximum effort of will they gave pleasure to an audience and made it laugh after it had forgotten how.

The hardships of the war and blockade were felt by everyone, but the very greatest difficulties fell to the women. Taking the places of men called up for duty, they worked in production and did housework too. In the care of home and children, no one could take their places. They followed the most stringent economies day by day (and in the course of each day, hour by hour) in apportioning the scanty food. They fetched wood with great trouble and used every scrap of it sparingly so that their children would not freeze. They would bring water in buckets from the nearest river. They did the laundry and mended clothes for the children and themselves by the dim light of oil lamps. Under the burden of the deprivation caused by the blockade and the dual responsibilities of jobs in industry and at home, the health of many women was seriously affected. Their will to live, their moral strength, resolution, efficiency, and discipline will always be the example and inspiration for millions of people.

Hunger revealed character. It laid bare hitherto undiscovered feelings and traits. The vast majority bore the hardships of hunger, physical pain, and mental distress bravely and stubbornly. They continued to work honestly, but there were others for whom the material well-being of ordinary times had concealed vices and weaknesses. Hunger's bony hand ripped off the protective covering and openly displayed the essence of each individual to his own surprise and that of the people close to him. Like oil stains on clean water, there appeared the egotists who would snatch bread from their own children, the thieves who would steal their neighbor's rations or take a sick woman's overcoat for a hundred grams of horse meat—and all the other parasites eager to build their own well-being on other people's grief. They stopped at nothing. The manager of a bread store of the Smolninsky *raion*, Akkonen, and her assistant, Sredneva, sold their customers bread at false weight. They would steal four or five grams of bread from each hunger ration and barter these for furs, antiques, and objects of gold. In the pursuit of profit, they had forgotten that they were still in a Soviet city. Although the city was encircled by fierce enemies, the laws of the revolution were preserved and respected. The crimes of Akkonen and Sredneva were discovered, and by sentence of the court, both were shot. The air had been cleared of something foul.

Hunger tormented people. All lived in the hope that soon, very soon, the Winter Road would be ready and food would start to arrive. Only a little while longer and there would be bread. As if in spite, the lake remained unfrozen and the days of waiting dragged wearily on.

8

THE WINTER ROAD

November, 1941–February, 1942

THE SECOND HALF OF NOVEMBER arrived. From the low, sloping shore of Lake Ladoga where the fishing village of Kokkorevo huddled under snow, the white plain of the lake stretched into the distance broken only by a dark strip of open water on the northeast. No barrier of water appeared to the southeast. Ice glittered as far as a delighted eye could see. Reconnaissance patrols with the aid of experienced fishermen cautiously began the crossing from the western to the eastern shore, measuring the

TABLE 23

Thickness of Ice (In mm.)	At −5° C. (Days)	At −10° C. (Days)	At −15° C. (Days)
100	2.7	1.4	0.9
150	6	3	2.1
200	11	5.5	3.6
300	24	12.3	8.2

thickness of the ice and placing markers for the future highway. According to the findings of specialists, formation of ice on Lake Ladoga proceeds at the rates given in Table 23. The rate of thickening depends on the length of the period of freezing at a particular average air temperature.

For the passage of freight across the ice, the thickness must be 100 millimeters for horses without a load; 180 millimeters for horses pulling a sledge bearing a load of one ton; and 200 millimeters to support a truck carrying a load of one ton.

The ice would have to be two hundred millimeters thick along the entire route to support a mass transportation of supplies. By November 17, ice on the lake was one hundred millimeters thick, insufficient to open operations.

Horse-drawn sledges, trucks, and tractors, ready for work, awaited a freeze. Workers of the highway service measured the ice at different parts of the lake several times each day but were powerless to speed its formation.

On the morning of November 18 the longed-for north wind began to blow; by the end of the day the temperature was down to $-12°$ and remained there for several days. On November 20 the thickness of the ice reached 180 millimeters. They could not force themselves to wait any longer. For safety's sake they began with horses and sledges only. The worn-out horses could hardly move; many fell and could not get up. These the drivers killed; then and there on the ice they cut them to pieces and sent the meat to the city.

And now came the bright day when machines began to move across the ice. On the morning of November 22, keeping intervals between them, at low speed, one truck after another went to pick up the long-awaited supplies along the tracks made by the horses. The column returned on November 23 with thirty-three tons of food. On the following day only nineteen tons were delivered. The fact that such small quantities of food were being delivered was the result of the brittleness of the ice, which was uneven along much of the route and quite thin in places. Two-ton trucks carried only two or three sacks each, and even with this precaution several machines went through the ice and sank. Nevertheless, spirits rose and the amount of traffic was increasing. In order to increase deliveries and prevent machines from breaking through the ice, sledges were attached to the truck. Three or four sacks were loaded on a machine and two or three on the sledge. This method of transportation decreased the pressure on the ice and made it possible to carry twice as much freight. Still the amount of food delivered was insignificant. Daily deliveries totaled 70, 154, 126, 196, and 128 tons for November 25–29, respectively.

On November 30 warmer weather set in. During the day the

temperature reached 0° or —1°, falling at night to —3° or —4°. That day only sixty-two tons were delivered.

From November 23 to December 1, inclusive, about eight hundred tons of flour were delivered by horse and machine—less than two days' requirement—and forty trucks sank or stuck in water holes. Traffic was curtailed owing to the fragility of the ice, although there was bread for only six days in the city, including the potential use of edible cellulose manufactured there.

With the weather so changeable, the ice did not build up, and the Military Council continued to face the same relentless question of what to do. Reduce the ration? Intolerable; it was pitifully small already and people were dying. They decided to appropriate the emergency supplies of flour aboard the special warships stationed around Kronstadt and to use the hardtack in the soldiers' emergency rations. The measure was extreme, but it was the only one that could prevent a complete halt in the distribution of bread. Their ration was a hunger ration, but still the inhabitants received bread every day. It may be imagined what would have happened if the population had ceased to receive bread even for two or three days in that time of crisis. As it was, the physical strength of the Leningraders was declining catastrophically.

On December 6, with the active help of the collective farms, the road to Zaborye Station bypassing Tikhvin was completed. By great exertion of will-power on the part of the soldiers and collective farmers, a road more than two hundred kilometers long was built under difficult conditions in a short time (although not within the prescribed time limit). The road went through rugged country; inhabited spots were rarely encountered. A considerable stretch of the road was too narrow for cars to pass each other; moreover, deep snow and steep grades on a road with which the drivers were unfamiliar led to frequent accidents and extremely slow traveling.

It so happened that three days after the completion of construction the military situation in the Tikhvin sector of the front changed sharply for the better, so that the road was used for only a few days. This greatly relieved the besieged city, since the road could not have kept the city and the Front alive for long; the rate of turnover during the first days of traffic over the new road was extremely low. A truck convoy sent from Zaborye to Novaya Ladoga returned fourteen days later, thus averaging thirty-five kilometers a day. On the section from Novaya Ladoga to Yeremina Gora alone, more than 350 trucks became stuck during the three days of traffic.

The experience of transporting freight from Voibokalo to Osinovets showed the enormous difficulties of making regular deliveries of even the insignificant amounts needed to supply the population and troops with food for their hunger rations; yet the route from Voibokalo was one-sixth as long and the road was incomparably better.

The events which improved the situation for those under siege occurred as follows. The Soviet General Staff was aware that with the loss of Tikhvin the position of Leningrad's defenders became more precarious every day and that if time were lost the Germans would fortify their positions, as happened at the beginning of September in the area of Mga-Sinyavino. A battle might then assume a protracted character. Supreme Headquarters gave orders to effect a concentration of troops under the command of General of the Army K. A. Meretskov, now Marshal of the Soviet Union, in the region of the Northern Railroad. The troops were assigned the objective of crushing the enemy forces which had driven a wedge into our defenses and liberating Tikhvin.

Knowing the strength of the enemy's grip on the town, Meretskov began cautiously and gradually to push in the flanks of the Fascist forces, and by the end of November his units reached the enemy's communications. Fearing encirclement, the Germans brought up strong reinforcements, but it was already too late. Still lightly clad owing to their leaders' lack of foresight and their failure to anticipate a winter campaign, the enemy troops suffered also from the very cold weather that had begun. On the night of December 9, Meretskov fell upon Schmidt's main forces with the whole strength of the troops intrusted to him and took Tikhvin by storm. The enemy left seven thousand dead on the battlefield and many guns, tanks, and smashed vehicles. Maintaining their pressure on the Germans, Soviet troops liberated a number of inhabited points in the area and threw the enemy back across the Volkhov River. An important communication center, after thirty days in the invader's hands, had been recovered.

It may be said without exaggeration that the defeat of the German-Fascist forces at Tikhvin and the recapture of the Northern Railroad as far as Mga saved thousands of people from death by starvation and strengthened the defense of Leningrad. The significance of this victory in terms of morale was even greater: the burden of uncertainty weighing upon the besieged dropped away, while the widely advertised success of the German army in capturing Tikhvin at the beginning of November—with the consequent expectation that Leningrad would soon fall—now gave place to a great decline in the prestige of the enemy army and to confusion on the part of Goebbels' unrestrained propaganda.

The route of the German forces at Tikhvin was no less crucial for the fate of Leningrad than the breaking of the blockade in January, 1943. On December 9 there remained for the city only enough grain for nine or ten days, including the flour at Novaya Ladoga. By this time, the oil cake, bran, mill dust, and other "reserves" had been completely consumed. People were so badly nourished that the death rate increased daily. Yet in order to maintain the existing December ration levels (in terms of actual consumption of food), nearly a thousand tons of provisions had to be delivered to the city every twenty-four hours. It was also necessary, however, to deliver gasoline, ammunition, and other important military supplies. Even with the finest organization of truck deliveries, it was hardly possible to bring in more than six or seven hundred tons a day from Zaborye Station of all kinds of freight. It is not hard to imagine the plight of the besieged in this situation. The liberation of Tikhvin must be rightfully regarded as a turning point in the defense of the city.

In certain books and articles on the blockade published during the war or many years later sometimes, annoying errors have been committed in treating specific events and facts which were of great significance in the history of the city's defense. Without analyzing each article on the question, I cannot forgo discussing the mistaken interpretation of the Tikhvin episode contained in E. Fedorov's book, *The Ice Road*.[1] The reader learns that "in November, in the hardest days, the Red Army attacked the troops of a German mechanized corps and routed it." Such an assertion is confusing because something else is well known: in the hardest days of November, when the bread supply was becoming exhausted, when a cold wave arrived and the lake was impassable, the enemy took and held Tikhvin for thirty days, and this situation brought in its train serious consequences for the besieged. According to Fedorov's interpretation, the enemy was routed in November and thus the loss and recovery of Tikhvin did not substantially affect the lives of the Leningraders. In the same book the following lines can be found:

> Three days passed. On January 11, 1942, Commissar Comrade Petrosian reported to the Chief of Military Automobile Roads: "The road is ready."
>
> While around the campfires the troops were cleaning up the last traces of the military encampment, such a stream of freight was already hurrying over the dirt highway as no forest road in the world has ever seen. The impassable Forest resounded with the noise of powerful machines carrying provisions to Leningrad.

Fedorov will find it hard to say where he discovered the forest road of January 11. It is perfectly well known, however, that after January 1, 1942, freight was delivered as far as Voibokalo by rail and that from this station it was transported on trucks as far as Lavrovo, a distance of twenty kilometers; there is no impassable forest along this stage of the journey and beyond stretches the lake. The amount of freight transported from Voibokalo, moreover, was very small. Not only could it not be displayed as an example to the "world," it completely failed to satisfy the Leningraders as will be recounted below.

Mistakes in the scholarly literature on the defense of Leningrad create the worst confusion, because large numbers of people use these books to study the subject. From them, they learn about the

[1] E. Fedorov, *The Ice Road* (Moscow: State Literary Publishing House, 1943).

past, draw their conclusions, and make their judgments of praise or blame. Mistakes in this literature are also dangerous because sometimes the authors seem to reassure the reader by their references in almost every sentence to primary sources. They seem to say: "Don't have any doubts; it's all true. It's all been checked in such and such an archive; that's exactly what it says in such and such a file," and the reader believes it.

Just this sort of mistake is made by F. I. Sirota in his book *Leningrad: Hero-City*.[2] "Although food supplies had increased they were very inadequate and quickly melted away. In order to achieve a more economical expenditure of food, a ration system was introduced as early as July 18 in Leningrad and its suburbs," the author writes on page 88.

This statement in itself is misleading because it permits the interpretation that the ration system was introduced only in Leningrad owing to special circumstances; actually, it was introduced on July 18 not only in Leningrad but also in Moscow and subsequently in other cities.[3]

Following the above quotation, Sirota gives the amount of food issued per person to the population of Leningrad. From these figures the reader learns that many inhabitants of this city, as early as July 18, received no other foods on their ration cards than bread, cereals, and sugar. The levels of distribution of food for all categories of workers are represented as much lower than they actually were. The author thus seems to confirm his thesis that Leningrad was in a special position. In order to dispel any doubt of the trustworthiness of his statistics, he refers to the Leningrad *Pravda* of July 18, 1941.

Reader, let us take the trouble to remove the newspaper, yellowed with age, from the archives, brush away the dust, and find

[2] F. I. Sirota, *Leningrad: Hero-City* (Leningrad: Leningrad Publishing House, 1960).

[3] The ration system for the workers of Leningrad and Moscow was introduced in both cities on July 18, 1941, by decision of the Soviet government. Identical amounts of food were issued in Moscow and Leningrad. The inhabitants of Leningrad received food according to this ration scale up through September, 1941 (amounts indicated on p. 79 of this book).

the reference we want. The rates of distribution of food supplies are actually given in the quantities indicated by Sirota, but the figures do not apply to the population of Leningrad. They refer to certain towns in Leningrad *oblast*. And this important fact the author did not notice, while mechanically applying to Leningrad the rates established for the inhabitants of Volkhov, Mga, Pargolovo, and Vsevolozhk, and thereby unintentionally committing a gross error, not to mention his incorrect explanation of the reasons why the ration-card system was introduced in Leningrad. A further justification for pointing out this mistake is that Sirota has written a number of works dealing with the defense of the city and must know very well that the rates of distribution of food to the inhabitants of Leningrad have been published in a number of books and that they differ quite significantly from those he gives in *Leningrad: Hero-City*.

Sirota asserts on page 93 of the book:

> During November of the first year of the war the majority of the inhabitants received 125 grams of bread per day. The amount of all other foods issued on ration cards fell to 920 grams per person per month. But it was not always possible to supply the population with even this scanty ration.

The author is guilty here of logical inconsistency in his characterization of the supply situation and a number of other errors. The bread rations varied in November. Until November 13 workers received 400 grams and all other categories of employees received 200 grams. From November 13 up to November 20 the minimum ration was 150 grams. Workers received 300 grams. Office workers, dependents, and children began receiving 125 grams only on November 20, at which time workers were allotted 200 grams. The general statement of a 125-gram bread ration for the majority of inhabitants during November is consequently incorrect and contradicts the table of bread rations given on page 92 of Sirota's book. The statement that the quantity of food per person fell to 920 grams per month is ambiguous. Is it supposed to apply to all categories of workers or only to some? If it is an average rate, how and by whom is it computed? The following words—"But it was not always possible to supply the population with even this scanty ration"—logically suggest that the scant ration amounted to 920 grams. In fact a dependent's card (the lowest category) was good for about two kilograms of food during November, and other categories received more. Although the population actually received something less than the stipulated amount of food, no ration card came to less than 1,500 grams, in addition to bread, in November, even on a dependent's card.

Even such a useful book as A. V. Karasev's *The Leningraders during the Years of the Blockade*[4] unfortunately contains occasional unfounded assertions. The author quotes data from an archive to support his statement on page 136: "In addition to cellulose, the bark of trees, leather scrapings, and other admixtures were added to the bread." Karasev has taken archival notes mechanically into a work of serious research without subjecting them to analysis. These admixtures (bark of trees and leather scrapings) were not used either for the population of the city or for the troops. Before any substitute could be used, it had to be discussed and approved by the Military Council and the City Party Committee. There are no decrees on these admixtures, and there were no such substitutes. I may add that it was my duty to take account of all food supplies and distribute them from the beginning of the blockade. Bark and leather scrapings were not recorded in the accounts and were not distributed for the same reason that the Military Council of the Front made no decision on them.

The author commits even more important errors when he writes on the same page that the population received no food other than a scanty piece of bread from November 20 on and that this day marked the beginning of the "hunger blockade" for Leningrad. The statement is striking but incorrect. Aside from bread, the population received other foods in December and at the end of November, in very small amounts to be sure. The meager rations kept many people alive somehow. In this connection, it must not be forgotten that the majority of the city continued to work. Peo-

[4] A. V. Karasev, *The Leningraders during the Years of the Blockade* (Moscow: Academy of Science of the USSR Publishing House, 1957).

ple would not only have been unable to work if they had received no food other than the current bread ration after November 20, but they would all have died of starvation. This did not and could not have happened because the food situation, although extremely precarious, was not as Karasev describes it.

The author's assertion that November 20 marks the beginning of the hunger blockade is unfortunate. The formulation suggests that the city's inhabitants experienced no shortage of food until that date. Food supplies actually diminished from the first days of the blockade, with the besieged purposely lowering ration levels to make food supplies last longer. Dystrophy appeared as early as November among such groups as dependents and office workers, and more than 11,000 persons died of starvation that month. The division of the blockade, therefore, into a "hunger period" after November 20 and another undefined period before November 20, as Karasev does, is artificial.

The ruined railroad bridges between Tikhvin and Volkhov had to be restored in order to relieve the situation of the besieged and bring victory closer. Railroad units of the People's Commissariat of Ways of Communications were assigned the construction work and immediately set about the task. While this work went on, the problem of transporting supplies from the eastern shore of Lake Ladoga to the city more quickly remained to be dealt with. Food deliveries were still unsatisfactory even on those days when the ice was firm and trucks did not fall through. The trouble lay in the bad organization of the transportation service. Drivers were not held responsible for specific vehicles, and as a result trucks were often out of service waiting for repairs. The repair service itself was most inefficient. The automobile battalions were subordinated to the road administration through a brigade headquarters which acted as an obstacle hampering operational direction. The road was not divided into sectors, telephone communication broke down regularly, and snow drifts, patches of open water, bomb craters, and dozens of other causes delayed traffic. The representative of the Rear Services of the Leningrad Front, Colonel Zhmakin, who was responsible for operating the automobile convoys, was not energetic and resourceful. He saw the cause of the whole trouble in the drivers' incompetence and took no action other than to demand that driver training be intensified. He did not notice how the absence of personal responsibility was a plague on the work of an organization numbering in the thousands and brought to nothing the fruitful labor of many people. His behavior called to mind a zealous teamster who readily climbs down from his wagon and, with all his strength and in the sweat of his brow, helps his horse pull a load uphill without ever realizing that someone has harnessed the horse wrong and the great effort is being expended in vain. Such a man was the honest and hardworking Zhmakin. The size of the job was plainly beyond his powers.

The Military Council and the City Party Committee, with their fingers on the city's pulse, understood the extreme danger that poor work by the road service posed to the defenders. Each hour in every day was precious. Steps had to be taken without delay to feed the city, for everything hung by a hair: the emergency supplies on the ships and the hardtack that was the soldiers' rations had been consumed.

Zhdanov and Kuznetsov rode out on the lake, studied the road, the work of the convoys, the way the drivers treated their machines, and realized the causes of the frequent accidents. After their return from the lake, the Military Council ordered the removal of Zhmakin as head of transportation; the elimination of the automobile brigade level of command; the direct subordination of the automobile battalions to the road commander; the marking of vehicles for assignment to particular drivers; the fixing of 2.25 tons per day as the normal haul for one machine of the GAZ-AA type with two drivers; the introduction of a specially devised bonus system for the drivers; and the division of the road into sectors for whose condition the road-command service would be responsible.

A blow was dealt the system of undefined responsibility. The advanced experience of the civilian economy was in large part carried over to the military management of the road. These measures improved transportation, although the population still had to live through many dark days and lose many dear ones before hunger was driven from the long-suffering city.

On December 22, seven hundred tons of provisions were delivered over the lake, and one hundred tons more than that the next day. The average daily delivery began to exceed daily expenditure. But the city and the Front continued to be fed directly from the trucks, and the slightest hitch in delivery would inevitably have produced a catastrophe. Nevertheless, on December 24, at Zhdanov's suggestion the Military Council, on the basis of the current situation and their confidence in the future, decided to increase the bread ration beginning December 25: for workers and engineer-technical workers by 100 grams; for office workers, dependents, and children by 75 grams.

So crucial an action as an increase in bread consumption when only the daily deliveries could be counted on, when there were no reserves to fall back on if deliveries broke down (which was not unlikely) seemed like a leap into the unknown with closed eyes. There is no worse mistake for a governing body than to announce a rash decision, that raises hopes and makes people happy, which it is then not able to carry out. But this did not happen. The calculation was accurate and fully justified. Tikhvin remained firmly in Soviet hands and our troops continued to push the Germans away from the railroad. Everything depended on the efficiency of transportation, on the initiative and enterprise of the workers on the Ice Road. But these difficulties had already been surmounted. The famished population needed immediate help, physical and moral. There comes an end to everything. Circumstances dictated that the slightest possibility, however uncertain, of improving the diet of the beseiged had to be exploited, and so it was done.

On December 25, as usual, the inhabitants went to the food stores early in the morning where they learned to their surprise that the bread ration had been increased. The joyful news circulated through the whole city with lightning speed. In spite of its being a cold day all who were able to walk left their homes to share in the general rejoicing. Streets and squares spontaneously filled with people, strangers embraced each other, shook hands, shouted "Hurrah," and wept tears of the triumph of life. An unforgettable day! The pale, gaunt faces smiled, and a light that had vanished reappeared in their eyes. In this small addition to their rations, people sensed the failure of the enemy blockade and a strengthening of the shaken forces of the besieged. It was the first important victory of the defenders of Leningrad. The new ration level was still far too low to satisfy the needs of the exhausted people and the population continued to go hungry, but every worker, every inhabitant, and soldier believed strongly that after the first increase there would soon be another.

In the novel *Baltic Sky*[5] by Nikolai Chukovsky a different date is given for the first increase in the bread ration, the increase is larger, and the circumstances are altered. I quote from the novel: "On the following day, January 24, the store issued Sonya not 125 grams of bread on her ration card but 250 grams." Then: "This was the first tangible gift of the Ice Road." To avoid disputes over one and the same fact, a fact that was of great significance in the life of the besieged, I quote the decision of the Military Council from the official record:

DECREE

OF THE

MILITARY COUNCIL OF THE LENINGRAD FRONT

No. 00493

Field Forces   December 24, 1941

Beginning December 25 of this year bread will be issued in accordance with the following ration scale:

Workers and engineer-technical workers	350 grams
Office workers, dependents, and children	200 grams

Commander of the Leningrad Front
Lt. Gen. KHOZIN

Member of the Military Council
Secretary, CC,ACP(b) ZHDANOV

The first increase in the bread ration took place on December 25, 1941, not January 24, 1942; the amount of increase in the ration of an office worker or a dependent was not 125 grams but

[5] N. Chukovsky, *Baltic Sky* (Moscow: "Soviet Writer" Publishing House, 1955).

75 grams. The Ice Road was still functioning extremely poorly at that time and could not give a "tangible gift," but raising the bread rations one month earlier than Chukovsky mistakenly asserts was of major importance. The increased bread ration in December saved many people, and the Leningraders remember it very well. Events of great significance in people's lives should not be treated "in passing." There was a second increase in the bread ration on January 24, made possible by satisfactory deliveries of food over the lake. From that day on workers received 400 grams, office workers 300 grams, dependents and children 250 grams a day. The author of the novel has confused both the time and amount of the increase and drawn from these mistakes the erroneous conclusion that only on January 24, 1942, was it "clear to all that the siege lines had been breached, that the city was no longer cut off from the rest of the country, and that the plan of the Hitlerites had not succeeded." In actual fact the population really sensed the failure of the enemy blockade from the day of the first increase in the bread ration, December 25, 1941.

Chukovsky, telling the stern truth about the defenders of Leningrad in his novel but wishing to bring out more vividly the difficulties of delivering provisions to the besieged, resorted to invention. He writes, for example: "They started to move the food across to Leningrad: a Red Army man would hitch himself to a sled and pull it to the other shore under the very noses of the Germans. They could not get all the way across during the day, so wherever they were they spent the night on the bare ice. You can't carry much across on a sled!"

In reality, such a way of transporting supplies was not used and could not have been. One need only calculate how many thousands of soldiers would have been required to carry just one day's supply of flour thirty kilometers across the lake on sleds and the absurdity becomes clear. There are no documents to confirm that Red Army men were used for this purpose, and there would have been documents if supplies had been so carried. Food was not delivered haphazardly by individuals. It was moved in a strictly organized way. Admittedly this is a small detail, but it is not true and it lowers the value of a good novel.

Invention is justified and permissible in artistic literature unless it contradicts historical truth or is substituted for it. The life of the Leningraders during the siege was so grim and their struggle so courageous that artists and writers need not "brighten the color or darken the shadow" in depicting the events of those years.

As a result of the faster transportation of food from Novaya Ladoga, the reserves created in October were used up and there were no supplies available at more distant points. No trains were arriving at Tikhvin, and a dangerous vacuum was forming between Tikhvin and Leningrad. This unexpected complication was caused by violent fighting on neighboring fronts. In the Yaroslavl-Rybinsk sector the railroad was choked with troop trains. This disastrous situation was reported to the government. On the same day the Military Council received an answer from A. I. Mikoyan, stating that the government had decided to send 50,000 tons of flour and 12,000 tons of other types of food immediately from the nearest supply centers and that freight trains would start to arrive at Tikhvin in three or four days; as soon as the restoration of railroad bridges had been completed the trains would be rerouted to Volkhov. Mikoyan told them not to worry about deliveries by rail because the People's Commissariat of Ways of Communication, despite the exceptional difficulties in railroad transport, would take steps to assure that trains for Leningrad ran on time.

Reassuring though this message was, it did not diminish the alarm of the Military Council and the city's leaders. Between directives even from a high level and their implementation there is much room for delays and obstruction, especially at a time of extreme cold weather with the railroad lines choked with trains and stations subject to raids by enemy aircraft. Meanwhile the consumption of bread went on without interruption. Every day saw the supplies of flour drop by 600 tons. The besieged could last no more than five days. The danger that the decision just made on December 24 to increase the bread ration would have to be rescinded was close upon them.

Three days of tense waiting passed before their apprehensions were dispelled. Trains loaded with flour and cereals began arriving one after the other. Numerous obstacles were overcome by the enthusiasm of the workers of Seima, Rybinsk, and Saratov. Millers did not go home until they had sent off the last train for Leningrad; when the men became exhausted, their wives took their places. On the cars the workers painstakingly printed inscriptions in big letters: "Food for Leningrad," and the railroad men let these trains through ahead of all the others, giving them the "green light." There can be no doubt also that the energetic and authoritative intervention of Mikoyan helped speed up deliveries of food. He kept his eye on the daily process of loading and dispatching trains, and if the slightest hitch occurred he participated personally in removing it.

At the end of December Tikhvin was like a gigantic ant hill. Around the clock thousands of workers and soldiers unloaded trains as they arrived and loaded what seemed to be an endless belt of trucks with various supplies. The loaded machines set out on the long journey by way of Koskovo–Kolchanovo–Syasstroi–Novaya Ladoga–Kabona–Ice Road–Osinovets. The vacuum was filled. The danger of a breakdown in provisioning receded, though it did not vanish because the amounts of food delivered to Leningrad were hardly enough for the new, still minimal, ration. The journey was a long one, more than 190 kilometers, and the road was bad. It was barely possible to make one trip in two days.

At the end of December the distance the trucks had to travel was reduced by one-third, and this greatly facilitated delivery of supplies. In successful fighting the Fifty-fourth Army pushed the Germans away from the railroad stations of Voibokalo and Zhikharevo which made it possible to deliver goods by truck from Tikhvin to Kolchanovo, reload them on trains, and at Voibokalo and Zhikarevo stations reload them on trucks. This combined means of transport (railroad–truck–railroad–truck) continued until January 1, 1942. (See Map 6.)

At five o'clock in the morning on New Year's Day through-train service from Tikhvin to Volkhov and Voibokalo began. This fine New Year's present came to the Leningraders from the railroad reconstruction units. From then on the truck run was on the short

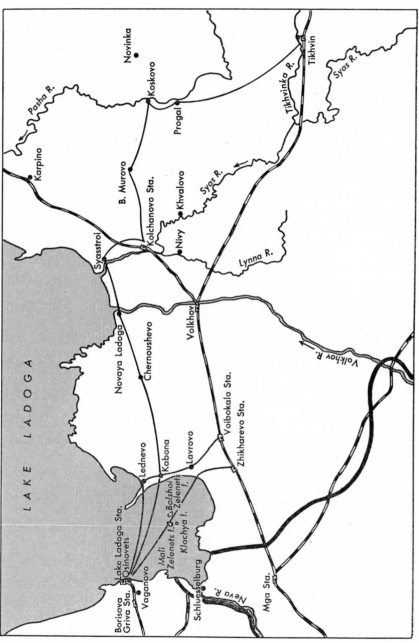

MAP 6.—Supplying Leningrad after the liberation of Tikhvin

side: 55 kilometers (Voibokalo–Lake Ladoga Station) instead of 320 kilometers to Zaborye and 190 kilometers to Tikhvin.

The route was now one-sixth what it had been, and still deliveries of food and other supplies were insignificant. From Voibokalo and Zhikharevo the trucks brought only small quantities of provisions. Snow storms and cold weather hindered traffic and, in addition, the road was not kept in working condition because of a shortage of snow-removal equipment. A long stretch of the road was too narrow for machines to pass each other without slackening speed. The drivers lacked experience in transporting freight over ice.

Again the Military Council took a series of supplementary steps to improve the movement of traffic. Four routes were established across the lake, two for loaded vehicles and two for empties:

First route, for loaded vehicles: Voibokalo–Lavrovo–Lake Ladoga Station; second, for empty vehicles: Lake Ladoga–Babanova–Voibokalo. Third route, for loaded vehicles: Zhikharevo–Troitskoe–Podal–Lavrovo–Lake Ladoga; fourth, for empty vehicles: Lake Ladoga–Lavrovo–Gorodishche–Zhikharevo Station.

To maintain them in working condition the routes were divided into company sectors with snow-removal equipment on permanent duty. The road from Tikhvin to Novaya Ladoga was closed on January 5, but to be on the safe side it was maintained in working condition. In view of the hard work of the drivers and traffic controllers on the lake, they were given a larger daily ration: bread, 500 grams; meat, 125 grams; fats, 40 grams; sugar, 35 grams; cereals, 190 grams; vodka, 50 grams. The trans-shipment base Voibokalo–Zhikharevo was removed from the authority of the Rear of the Leningrad Front and subordinated to the road commander.

To help the administration of the Front-Line Road, industrial enterprises assigned transport and laborers to it. Several hundred specialists and party and Soviet workers headed for the road. Through personal example, by the care with which they did their work, they served as models for the many thousands in the army of road workers.

The question arose of appointing the commander of this vital artery. The majority of the members of the Military Council proposed Major General Shilov of the supply service, who had experience in moving cargoes by water and had displayed administrative talents in directing large groups of people. When the appointment was suggested to Shilov, he thought it over for a while because he knew the difficulties that beset the road and understood how great his responsibility to the country would be. Most of all he hesitated because he was not sure he was strong enough to bear the burden. Then he went up to Zhdanov and reported in military style that he would accept the appointment and was proud of the honor. Noting Shilov's emotion, Zhdanov embraced him: "I can understand your concern and I prize your decision." Shilov proved equal to the task allotted him, showing great skill in managing the road during the whole period of the siege. There is no doubt that he made a significant contribution to Leningrad's defense capabilities by his work.

In this critical period for the fate of the city, Zhdanov sent a letter to the personnel of the road:

Dear Comrades:

The front-line automobile road continues to function very badly. Every day it delivers no more than a third of the supplies necessary to satisfy, even in the slightest degree, the needs of Leningrad and the troops for food and gasoline although these needs have been cut to the absolute minimum. This means that the provisioning of Leningrad and the Front is always hanging by a hair and the population and the troops are suffering incredible privations. This is all the more intolerable because supplies for Leningrad and the Front are on hand. So it is up to you, workers of the front-line road, and only you to improve the situation quickly and relieve the need of Leningrad and the Front.

The heroic defenders of Leningrad, protecting our city with honor and glory from the Fascist bandits, have the right to demand honorable and selfless labor from you.

On behalf of Leningrad and the Front I ask you to realize that you have been assigned a great and responsible task and are performing an assignment of paramount national and military importance.

Everyone on whom the normal functioning of the road depends: drivers, traffic controllers, snow removers, mechanics,
signal men, commanders, political workers, workers of the
Road Administration, each one must do his duty at his post
like a soldier in a forward position.

Get to work as Soviet patriots should, honestly, putting
your heart into it, not sparing your strength, not delaying a
single moment, so that supplies for Leningrad and the Front
can be delivered in the amounts prescribed by the plan.

The Motherland and Leningrad will never forget your
work!

Every word of this moving appeal went to people's hearts and
roused their strength for battle with the elements and the shortages. The skilful combination of major executive measures de-
signed to improve the operation of the truck road with the appeal
to drivers, workers, commanders, political workers, and all personnel played a decisive part in increasing deliveries. The road
units, overcoming the difficulties caused by a severe winter, constructed six routes across the lake in a short time to eliminate
two-way traffic; the drivers competed with each other to see who
could make two or three round trips a day. They began to clear
snow from the road systematically; when crevices formed they
laid prefabricated bridges of logs over them which were safe and
did not slow the pace of traffic. Tractors, graders, wooden angle
bars, and other equipment were procured and put at the disposal
of the Road Administration.

Within a few days the carrying capacity of the front-line road
increased. Now more than fifteen hundred tons of supplies were
delivered every day from the eastern to the western shore. The
surge in transportation encouraged the hope of a rapid improve-
ment in supplying the population, but trouble, as usual, developed. The Irinovsk Railroad from Osinovets to Leningrad, the
supply artery of the blockaded city, was incapable of running
even one train per day over a distance of fifty-five kilometers.
Freight piled up at Lake Ladoga Station, while Leningrad was
still going through days of torment, food had to be distributed on
arrival, and bread plants had flour for only one or two days.

In peacetime one train a day arrived at Lake Ladoga Station. Since there was need for no more, the station was not well equipped; it even got along without a pump house. Its storage facilities were small and sidings limited. And now a burden was unexpectedly dumped on this wretched baby of a station: six or seven trains a day in each direction, a load that only a well-developed railroad center could handle. Moreover, there was insufficient fuel and water for the engines along the route; at a number of stations the pump houses were out of commission owing to the very cold weather. What was necessary now, of course, was a thorough reconstruction of the Irinovsk road and the Lake Ladoga Station. To do this required time, whereas people must eat every day. While the state of affairs demanded that trains rush at twice their normal speed, they were standing still or hardly moving. Reproaches and threats rained down on the railroad men, but what hurt them most of all was their own inability to do their duty. It often happened that employees and workers at a station had their hands frostbitten carrying buckets of water to the locomotive tender so the train could move on to its destination. Train crews went into the woods to cut down trees and fueled the locomotives with damp, frozen wood that sputtered but did not burn. Lacking power, the trains stood still or moved at a speed of ten or twelve kilometers an hour with the help of two locomotives. Quantities of damp wood would be burned up, but the pressure would drop and there would begin the endless and frequent stops to get up more steam. In order to speed up traffic locomotives were kept on duty and ready to move at several stations. As soon as a train arrived, its engine was replaced by the engine on duty which had previously been fueled with dried wood. This practice required a large number of locomotives but moved the trains considerably faster. The engineers, firemen, and conductors of the freight trains were give an increase of 125 grams in their bread ration to maintain their strength as they performed this important and difficult work.

Food supplies arriving at Osinovets went into the general reserve no matter what their original destination had been and were distributed to military and civilian organizations by the Repre-

sentative with Full Powers of the State Defense Committee. The
system violated the usual accounting methods. When the Rybinsk
mills, for example, sent flour to the Leningrad branch of the State
Grain Purchasing Office, the bill for payment was presented to
the branch office which, however, had neither received nor distributed the flour and did not even know where it was. But under
the conditions this was the only correct way to distribute supplies. The supplies were kept together and could be sent at any
time where they were most needed. Trucks and storage places
handled maximum loads and the turn-around of freight cars rose.
The workers had many kinds of work to do and were equally busy
all the time. Financial accounts with the supplying agencies were
handled by the supply service of the Front. From their place of
dispatch, supplies were brought as far as Voibokalo Station by
rail and signed over to the front-line trans-shipment base. Here
the chain of responsibility for keeping the supplies intact was
broken, for during the next stage of transportation it was impossible to weigh every item being loaded on a truck. The time for
this would have kept many vehicles standing idle during loading
and unloading, and all the efforts of the Military Council and the
workers of the road service to accelerate truck turn-arounds
would have amounted to nothing. Supplies were loaded by visual
estimate; weight was determined by the number of sacks or boxes.
Accounting was simplified to the utmost: the driver's name, type
of load, and the number of items were entered on a printed receipt. With this document the driver set off on an assigned route,
from which he was forbidden to deviate. On arrival at his destination, he turned over the supplies, again without their being
weighed, but with the number of items checked against the number on the receipt. The system made it possible for certain dishonest drivers to steal food during the trip, either for personal
needs or to sell on the side. There were times when flour or cereals
were poured out of sacks or when canned goods, fruit, and chocolate were stolen from boxes. Since the number of boxes or sacks
tallied with the figure shown on the receipt, the driver could not
be held responsible for any losses because the food was badly
packed. The sacks were made of thin, patched cloth; much flour

sifted out, and the boxes, knocked together slipshod from thin planks, often broke or could easily be opened. With this kind of packing it was almost impossible to distinguish theft from loss.

The road workers, political workers, guards, traffic controllers, and drivers looked after the safety of the supplies. Those caught stealing were removed from work on the road immediately and brought to justice. But the most potent means of influencing such people turned out to be public opinion. Shame at the thought of their comrades quelled the temptation to profit by some dainty morsel loaded unweighed in the rear of a truck and with its packing almost open. Although there were comparatively many petty thefts at the beginning, it was not long before they stopped completely. Supplies were delivered over the winter road until the end of its existence with great care and precautions against losses.

Transporting supplies to the field forces during the siege of Leningrad and throughout the war on other fronts showed the great harm done to the national economy through the faulty packing of goods. It can be said without exaggeration that losses from scatterage, leakage, and spoilage during the war years came to many millions of rubles. Hundreds of tons of the most valuable products were strewed over innumerable roads.

Owing to a shortage of fat-proof oil paper, food concentrates were often wrapped in ordinary paper or newspaper. In these cases up to 20 per cent of the fat called for in the concentrate formula was absorbed by the paper. Losses of granulated sugar transported in sacks that had been used repeatedly were more than twice as large as losses incurred when new sacks were used. For a long time shag (*makhorka*) was not packed in containers and transported in boxes but was poured like grain into sacks. A result of the paper shortage, the practice led to much spillage. This kind of packing played into the hands of whatever dishonest people were involved in the transportation, storing, or distribution of shag; moreover, in wet weather shag so packed absorbed moisture and increased in weight, another factor exploited by the dishonest.

Industrial plants frequently filled freight cars with bulk loads of separate cans, if they were not supplied with packing materials in time. This oversimplified method resulted in losses, great expenditures of labor, and much idling of transport while the cans were unloaded onto trucks for delivery to army or divisional supply depots.

When the siege began, the Front Military Council sent the secretary of the Leningrad *Oblast* Party Committee, T. F. Shtykov, to the central regions of the country. He was assigned responsibility for the delivery of food and other supplies to Leningrad. With the active help of local Party organizations, Shtykov successfully carried out this important assignment. Deliveries of food, coal, fuel, ammunition, and other supplies to Leningrad were made from several hundred railroad stations scattered over the gigantic expanses of our country. Difficulties of one kind or another frequently arose at the loading points: now there would be a shortage of hands for loading, now of trucks and horses to haul the goods from the warehouses to the freight cars. Some stations might be covered with snow and need large numbers of people to clear their roads, and where was the labor force to be found when every man was already at his post? Sometimes trains stood idle on the sidings without enough coal for the locomotive; in short, the causes preventing prompt fulfilment of assignments were not few. Telegrams went to such stations from Moscow demanding immediate loading and the dispatch of the cars, but in these situations the messages did not always help matters. Shtykov, however, would hurry to the dispatching point and establish direct liaison with local authorities and public organizations; only with their active help would he be able to remove the causes obstructing the departure of goods for Leningrad. His vivid description of the life and struggle of the Leningraders stirred up the people; every man, no matter how tired he was after the working day, hurried to help Leningrad. Delivery followed delivery to the eastern shore of Lake Ladoga.

On January 20, 1942, the city's food supplies were as given in Table 24 (in tons).

These figures show the small amount of food in Leningrad, although on the near approaches to the city the amount of supplies had built up.

The Military Council and the city authorities knew when they made the first increase in the bread rations that they faced a struggle with snow drifts, ice hummocks, and the many other difficulties of a hard winter. In order to maintain the ration levels introduced December 25 much had to be done to improve the road and the safety of the deliveries and, first of all, to train personnel and organize traffic so that drivers would not be looking for the road on the boundless stretches of the deserted lake during the long nights, the blizzards, and the gloomy, short winter days.

A month of stubborn work went by. The drivers, the traffic controllers, the repair men, the communications people gained experience and confidence in their work. At any time of day or night, in snow storms and cold, they saw to it that convoys or

TABLE 24

	Flour	Cereals	Meat	Fats	Sugar
In warehouses in Leningrad.....	2,106	326	243	94	226
At Lake Ladoga Station........	2,553	690	855	130	740
En route from Lake Ladoga Station to Leningrad............	1,020	210	220	108	90
At Voibokalo-Zhikharevo.......	6,196	846	1,347	368	608
Total....................	11,875	2,072	2,665	700	1,664
Number of days' supply in terms of current ration levels........	21	9	20	9	13

individual trucks got through without risk of falling into open patches of water or bomb craters. Six routes, cleared and smoothed, stretched from one end of the lake to the other. Good roads and traffic safety enabled deliveries of food to Leningrad to be increased greatly, which in turn made it possible to maintain the first increase in the bread ration and even to increase the ration a second time and for the troops as well as the civilian population.

The new bread ration was introduced on January 24, 1942. Workers began to receive 400 grams, office workers 300 grams, dependents and children 250 grams, front-line troops 600 grams, and rear units 400 grams. And after a few days, on February 11, the bread ration was increased again.

The Winter Road over the ice across Lake Ladoga—the "Life Road" as the people called it—became busier every day. Trucks stretched in an endless ribbon in both directions. The German-Fascist forces observed the construction of the road and the increasing traffic over it; they bombed and shelled it as hard as they could without result; their bombs pierced the ice and exploded at the bottom, and the blast wave could not smash the ice. Craters made by bombs and shells were marked immediately by men of the road service, using long poles topped by fir branches. These could be seen from a distance, and the drivers detoured around them in time.

Aside from bombing raids and the shelling from long-range guns, the Germans attacked with fighter aircraft. The fighters came down low to pour machine-gun fire into the trucks, often causing damage and delays in traffic. Soviet aircraft came to the rescue: fighters constantly patrolled over the road, making it impossible for the Fascist fliers to swoop down. The days when enemy fighters had superiority in speed were over.

One cold January night about two companies of Fascist troops on skis, wearing white cloaks, tried a sortie from the Schluesselburg area over the lake to Osinovets for purposes of sabotage and reconnaissance. Under cover of falling snow they succeeded in penetrating several kilometers over the lake and reached the road; there they were discovered and hastily retreated with losses. This Fascist sortie in great depth showed the feasibility of a hostile thrust from the lake, if not at Osinovets itself then at the line of communications. To avert the danger the Front command assigned a special unit to guard the road. Along the lake near the south shore, machine-gun positions were established, protected by blocks of ice and snow. The soldiers lay on straw mats with chemical heaters in their pockets. Conditions were very difficult for the defenders on the bare surface of the ice; the freezing wind pierced them to the bone and there was no shelter, but enemy access was tightly sealed off. The battle of the Winter Road was finally won by the heroic efforts of Soviet soldiers.

Here it will be in order to sum up the amount of food supplies brought across the lake by various means of transportation from the beginning of the blockade to January 1, 1942. The data are given in Table 25 (in tons).

In addition to food, considerable quantities of ammunition, fuel, and other supplies were delivered during the same period of time. It should also be remembered that deliveries were being made simultaneously with the construction of the port at Osinovets and the deepening of the lake bottom so ships could be berthed there; barges were being repaired, blown bridges were being restored, and a road was being built over the ice. Under these circumstances the delivery of 45,685 tons of provisions reflects the heroic deeds and hard labor of thousands of Soviet

TABLE 25*

	By Water	By Air	Winter Road	Total
Grain, Flour....................	23,041	743	12,353	36,137
Cereals.........................	1,056	......	1,482	2,538
Meat and Meat Products...........	730	1,829	1,100	3,659
Fats, Cheese....................	276	1,729	138	2,143
Condensed Milk..................	125	200	158	483
Powdered Eggs, Chocolate Powdered Milk, etc.......................	......	681	44	725
Total	25,228	5,182	15,275	45,685

* Accounting figures of Rear Service, Leningrad Front, for 1941.

people. For it was through their efforts that the southern shore of Lake Ladoga, without harbors or mooring facilities, was converted in a brief period of time by the will of the Bolsheviks into a mighty artery nourishing the city and the Front.

The winter sun began to appear more often in the cheerless skies over Lake Ladoga. Spring was not far away, and with its coming the Winter Road would necessarily collapse under the pressure of awakening waters. A feeling of alarm and anxiety as to how the town was to be supplied grew every day. The ice would melt in three months, and a reserve had not yet been created that would carry through even the spring thaw. Here was something to ponder on. The autumn period of bad roads had brought too much grief and sacrifice not to teach them some lessons.

To build up small reserves while supplying the current needs of the population and the troops required that deliveries of supplies be doubled during the short time remaining. For this it would be necessary either to double the number of vehicles or decrease the distance they traveled by half. Since every available truck was already used to full capacity, the possibility of increasing the number of vehicles was excluded. The truck run could be shortened by extending the railroad to the edge of the lake, but this daring scheme—to build a rail line under winter conditions and in the immediate vicinity of the enemy—seemed impracticable. Nevertheless, after going through all the alternatives, it was decided to construct a branch line from Voibokalo Station to Kabona. When the Front Military Council presented its plan to build a line linking the eastern shore of the lake with the country's railroad system, the government gave its approval and assigned the work of construction to the People's Commissariat of Ways of Communication. Construction of the line began amid the snows and cold of winter and before the very eyes of the Germans.

By a titanic effort on the part of workers, technicians, engineers, and reconstruction units, a railroad thirty-four kilometers long was built and opened for operation February 10. Now trains could run right up to the lake. The quiet lake village of Kabona and its environs resounded to locomotive whistles, while over a large area around the village there arose hastily built warehouses, sheds, and dumps, surrounded by wire, with mountains of sacks of cereals, flour, and grain. Trucks left Kabona in an endless stream, hurrying to deliver their loads to the opposite shore. By shortening the truck run by thirty kilometers in one direction, the whole run was decreased by more than half. Round trips speeded up and deliveries increased, while fuel consumption dropped by 200 tons per day. The new branch line was of the greatest assistance to Leningrad not only during the winter but in summer as well.

On January 22 the State Defense Committee by special decree ordered the evacuation of 500,000 people from Leningrad. To carry out this decision, Deputy Chairman of the Council of Ministers of the USSR A. N. Kosygin arrived in the besieged city. The massive evacuation of the population began as soon as the winter road over the lake could handle it. First priority in evacuation was given to children, women, the aged, and the sick. What could not be done in July and August, 1941, was successfully undertaken during the winter and spring of 1942. There was no need to explain matters to the people: life had taught them much.

In January they evacuated 11,296 people; in February, 117,434 people; in March, 221,947 people; and in April, 163,392 people. In all, during less than a full four months, 514,069 people were evacuated over the Winter Road.

The spring thaw interrupted traffic over the lake. In the second half of May evacuation of citizens recommenced by water. From May through November, 1942, 448,010 persons were evacuated, and with this evacuation ceased.

The evacuation was carefully thought out and well organized. A series of field messes was set up on the road for the evacuees. As soon as the Leningraders crossed over the lake and reached land, they were served hot cabbage soup, soup with potatoes and meat, and other nourishment such as these exhausted people had dreamed of night after night. The fragrance of bread made from pure rye flour intoxicated the famished people. From their first step on land they were surrounded by loving care. Everyone felt in his heart the desire to help them in any way he could.

Kosygin also devoted much attention to evacuating valuable and rare machinery not being used in Leningrad at the time. From January through April, 1942, several thousand different machine tools and other types of machinery were evacuated over the road to the east of the country where they were sorely needed. These machines brought life to many a reassembled factory. Industrial plants picked up speed in producing the equipment necessary for routing the Fascist armies.

The needs of the Front and the city demanded thousands of tons of kerosene, gasoline, and oil, for which there were not enough oil tankers. Tanks were filled with fuel and floated across, but even this effective method of water transportation did not solve the problem of supplying a huge city with fuel. The Front Military Council, after thoroughly analyzing the proposals of a group of specialists, decided to lay an oil pipeline under the lake. When the project had been worked out in detail, it was submitted to the government of the USSR for examination and confirmation. The State Defense Committee approved it on April 25, 1942.

Soon specialists and trainloads of pipes, materials, and machines began to arrive at the eastern shore of Lake Ladoga. Laying the pipeline started under most difficult conditions. Through the efforts of an experienced crew from the Special Underwater Work Organization, military units, and workers, the construction of a pipeline about thirty kilometers long was completed on June 16, 1942.

With the pipeline operating, there was one more serious breach in the enemy blockade. Leningrad began to receive fuel in the necessary amounts the year round. The wheels of industrial life turned with increasing speed, and the mighty productive potential of the city revived. Leningrad, which had been written off by many people abroad under the influence of Goebbels' propaganda, stood proudly and gained strength. Time began to work again in favor of the besieged; the city became an even stronger fortress with dependable supplies of food, fuel, and ammunition. The pulse of productive activity beat stronger every day.

How could the Germans permit a branch line to be built to Kabona, a pipeline to be laid across the lake, and a massive evacuation of the population and heavy ship traffic, when these measures wrecked their plans to strangle the city by the blockade? The answer is that the Germans did not remain passive observers of the tireless activity of the Soviet people hurrying to the help of the besieged. The Fascists were furious; they dropped mines in large numbers, including magnetic mines, on the shipping routes, attempted landing operations from barges and launches transferred from the North Sea, and bombed Kabona, Osinovets, and the transports themselves. In 1942 during the spring and summer alone, the enemy flew about 5,000 sorties against the Ladoga route. The Germans fired at the frail barges with countless guns and dropped depth bombs to destroy the pipeline. Their attempts often attained their objectives, and the defenders suffered heavy losses, but the enemy did not succeed in frustrating the boldly conceived plans that were carried to completion by the persistent labor of Soviet people at Lake Ladoga and that played an exceptionally important part in the eventual rout of the Fascist troops at Leningrad.

Years will pass, and from every corner of the world people will be drawn to the shore of far-away Lake Ladoga to do homage to the great city and see with their own eyes the legendary "Life Road," to understand better the conditions under which the besieged waged their struggle. The road from Leningrad to Lake Ladoga, where death was overhead every minute and the prowess of thousands of people was so clearly displayed, will surely be a living page of the history of the Leningraders' struggle. The time will come when every kilometer of the way, through its memorial monuments, will tell all who travel the road of the hard days of the blockade, about the privations of the besieged and their terrible sufferings from hunger, about those who perished in the cause of a full and equal life for man, and about the triumph of victory over the ferocious enemy of humanity: fascism.

It is impossible to pass over in silence the regrettable fact that the Leningrad Defense Museum, opened soon after the war, was unjustifiably closed in 1949. Extremely rich materials were concentrated in the Museum to depict the heroic struggle of the besieged, the living conditions in Leningrad during the fearful days of blockade, and the defense measures against air raids and artillery bombardments. The great efficiency displayed by the workers in turning out weapons and building fortifications around and inside the city was shown, the battle against fires, the disarming of delayed-action bombs, and there were many other features to bring out the inventiveness, determination, and high courage of simple people. But the Museum was founded in the years when the cult of personality flourished, when many of the heroic deeds of the Leningraders were ascribed undeservedly to single individuals. Even in 1949, however, it was not hard to correct the mistakes engendered by the cult of personality and preserve the Museum, but, unfortunately, that was not what happened. The struggle carried on by Soviet people in the Fatherland War can, of course, be given a memorable description in other ways than through museums. While the arsenal of ways to immortalize their heroic deeds is rich and varied, and our nation holds sacred the memory of the heroic defenders of Leningrad, the feats of labor performed by the workers, and the courageous behavior of the whole population, the value of a museum, too, as a potent instrument for educating the masses should not be underestimated.

In 1957 the Leningrad Museum of History was opened. Several rooms are allotted to an exhibition illustrating the defense of the city during the Great Fatherland War. But these reflect only in small measure that memorable heroic epic. The exhibits are poor; they do not throw light on the military operations of the troops of the Leningrad Front and the Baltic Fleet. The struggle of the besieged with hunger is shown sketchily, and there is not even a corner for a collection of literature devoted to the life of the besieged and the defense of the city; there are many other annoying omissions. But the stream of visitors is large and among them are some who defended the city with their own bodies and some whose valorous labor strengthened its defense and some who helped the Leningraders in the difficult days of the siege from the different towns and villages of our motherland. Young people are especially numerous, and there are many visitors from other countries. They all want to see and imprint upon their memories the heroic past and the unexampled fortitude of the city's defenders.

Our contemporaries and many future generations will be infinitely grateful to those persons and organizations who can depict in the best manner and more fully all that helps youth to see clearly the physical, moral, and spiritual strength of its forebears and to hand these qualities on from generation to generation, all that glorifies our motherland and people, all that will find a response in the very bottom of every person's heart, all that preserves the memory of the deeds of those who died rather than bend their necks before the foreign invaders, and with their lives defended the honor and glory of Leningrad.

9

CONCLUSION

ONE SOMETIMES HEARS the questions asked: Why did the siege of Leningrad last so long? Was everything possible done to break the blockade earlier? In order to answer these questions, it is necessary to review the military operations around Leningrad, not separately, but in connection with the general course of the war along the entire Soviet-German front.

At the outset of the war, as we know, the Germans launched a rapid offensive against the Soviet Union in three sectors: northern, central, and southern. The enemy committed his main forces in the central sector with the objective of seizing the capital and thereby breaking the resistance of the Soviet state. Advancing on Moscow were fifty enemy divisions with large quantities of armor. In October the Germans transferred their Fourth Panzer Army from Leningrad to the central sector in an attempt to overcome the Soviet troops before Moscow by superior force.

On October 19 Moscow was declared to be in a state of siege. Despite heavy losses, forward units of the enemy were approaching the outskirts of the city. German newspapers and radio announced: "The German offensive against the Bolshevik capital has advanced so far that already it is possible, with a good pair of binoculars, to see inside the city."

The most serious danger impended. To avert it, the reserves of fresh troops that had been accumulated in the interior had to be concentrated at Moscow. Although other fronts—Leningrad especially—needed reinforcements, to have dispersed forces at such a time would have meant weakening the sector where the danger to the country was greatest.

With its reserves concentrated, the Supreme Command dealt the enemy a smashing blow at the decisive point for the campaign of 1941. The frontal attack on the capital ended in a major German defeat. On December 6 Soviet troops of the Western Front launched a counteroffensive that drove the enemy westward almost all winter and destroyed a large number of his men and much equipment. To halt the counteroffensive Hitler's headquarters was compelled to bring up and expend substantial army reserves that had been intended for the summer offensive.

While bringing about this strategic rout of enemy forces, the government did not for a moment forget Leningrad. Aware of the great importance to the besieged of the Northern Railroad— a long stretch of which had been taken by the enemy—the Soviet command ordered an attack in the vicinity of Tikhvin under the difficult conditions existing at the end of November. Once the town had been liberated, food and other supplies could be brought to Leningrad by rail from as near a point as possible. The operations of the troops of the Volkhov and Northwestern Fronts pinned down the enemy and at the same time substantially relieved the situation of Leningrad. But to break the blockade in 1941 would have required a major diversion of troops from other fronts, and this was impossible for the reason given above.

The German command could not accept the collapse of its plans and its defeat at Moscow and began feverishly to prepare for a new offensive. In April, 1942, Hitler issued a directive ordering that "as soon as the weather and terrain become favorable, the German High Command and the German armed forces must again seize the initiative in their hands in order to impose our will upon the enemy." It continued:

> The objective is to destroy the remaining Soviet defense potential and to cut them off as much as possible from their most important sources of supply. To achieve this, it is planned to maintain our positions in the central sector; in the north, to bring about the fall of Leningrad. . . . and on the southern flank to force a breakthrough into the Caucasus. . . .

> At the beginning of the campaign all available forces must be united for the main operations in the southern sector, whose objective is to destroy the enemy on this side of the Don in order to reach the oil regions of the Caucasus and cross the Caucasus mountains. . . . We must try to reach Stalingrad or at least bring it under fire from our heavy artillery to such an extent that it will henceforth be destroyed as a production center for arms and as a transportation center.

Through the transfer of almost all their forces to the Soviet-German front, the Germans had seventy more divisions there at the start of their summer offensive in 1942 than when they had attacked the Soviet Union the previous summer. Lavishly, the Fascist government rewarded its generals and other officers with promotions and various decorations, thus raising the fighting spirit of the officer corps and kindling it with aspirations to climb the service ladder. On June 30, 1942, in a special order, Hitler noted the great work of Kuechler, the commander of Army Group North, and promoted him to field-marshal general for his successful blockade of Leningrad. He fanned the dying spark of hope among Kuechler's soldiers that they would capture this most important Russian industrial center.

When the main German forces had been concentrated in the southwestern sector in accordance with Hitler's directive, the German Fascist command launched their troops in a wide offensive across the Russian plain. By the end of August the enemy had succeeded in advancing a great distance. Exerting every effort, they were attempting to cut off Soviet field forces from the Volga and the Urals, deny them their sources of supply, destroy their defense plants, break the Soviet Army's will to resist, and achieve the victory.

Naturally, the general situation during this time was exceptionally tense. Our main forces were directed against the principal enemy grouping, and here—at Stalingrad—the outcome of the German campaign of 1942 was decided at the culminating point of the great battle. As the fighting developed, the Fascist leadership brought in more and more divisions from other sectors. Even so they could not take Stalingrad. In the period from the middle of November to the beginning of December, 1942, Soviet troops encircled the main enemy concentration; during January and the beginning of February, 1943, they crushed them, breaking the German front and launching an offensive that threw the Germans hundreds of kilometers to the west. Hitler's Supreme Command attempted to stop the powerful Soviet offensive by transferring divisions from all sectors to the south.

Exploiting the favorably developing situation, the troops of the Volkhov and Leningrad fronts, strengthened with reserves made available by Supreme Headquarters, attacked the enemy's fortified positions south of Lake Ladoga from two sides. Resistance collapsed. The sixteen-month blockade was broken by the efforts of Soviet soldiers on January 18, 1943.

In order to give substantial help to the population and defenders of the city as quickly as possible, the government took measures to build a rail line at forced speed through the corridor of the breakthrough. In just eighteen days a line fifty kilometers long was laid and a temporary railroad bridge constructed across the Neva. (See Map 7.) As soon as a direct railroad link to the rest of the country was established, the supply situation improved sharply. Coal was delivered; industry received electricity. The frozen plants, factories, and streetcars revived. The city began to regain the strength it had lost for a while.

The general situation on the Soviet-German front remained tense, however, and enemy forces at Leningrad could not yet be completely crushed. Although the German army was in a state of major decline after the defeat at Stalingrad, it had not lost its capacity to continue the war. Moreover, the Fascist government of Germany was mobilizing all its remaining human and material resources and again preparing to launch a decisive blow at the Soviet forces.

In 1943 Hitler determined to pour all his aggressive fury into an offensive from the German bridgeheads at Orel and Belgorod. His plan was to smash the troops of the Central and Voronezh Fronts in the so-called Kursk Bend and open the way to his desired objective: Moscow. Concentrating great numbers of troops equipped with the powerful new "Tiger" and "Panther" tanks,

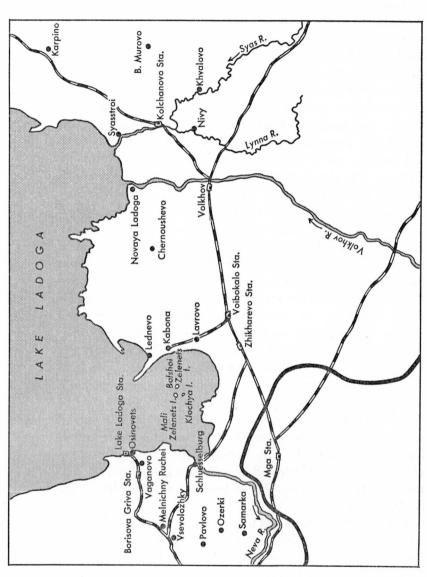

MAP 7.—Rail connections with Leningrad after the breaking of the blockade

"Ferdinand" self-propelled guns, "Panzerfaust" antitank projectiles, and other deadly weapons, Hitler's headquarters threw them into an offensive at the beginning of July, 1943. The Soviet command had, however, learned in advance not only the plan of the offensive but the very hour it would begin. The advantage of surprise was lost. In a stubborn, bloody battle the enemy army was utterly defeated. Following the defeat of the main German forces at Kursk, the Soviet army won a series of other victories. By the end of 1943, the military situation had changed radically. Along the whole front, our troops were preparing decisive new blows against the enemy.

At Leningrad, the Fascist German divisions remained in their positions, and Kuechler still counted on taking the beleaguered city.

But here, too, the day of reckoning was at hand. Under the command of Marshal Govorov the troops of the Leningrad Front, well trained and equipped, began an offensive in mid-January, 1944, from the areas of Oranienbaum and Pulkovo. The forts and warships of the Baltic Fleet opened a hurricane of fire on the fortified German positions. Simultaneously, the enemy was attacked by the entire force of the Volkhov Front. These troops enveloped Novgorod from the north and south and advanced on Luga, cutting the enemy's communications. The active operations of the Second Baltic Front, begun prior to the offensive of the Leningrad and Volkhov fronts, pinned down enemy reserves and prevented their transfer to Leningrad. As a result of this plan, carefully worked out by talented commanders and executed with well-organized co-operation by the troops of three fronts and the Baltic Fleet, an extremely powerful German force was routed and Leningrad freed completely from blockade.

Leningrad held out through such a prolonged siege, first of all, because the population—reared on the traditions of the Revolution and devoted to the last breath to its socialistic motherland and Communist party—fought to the death in defense of the city. The whole country, the entire Soviet people gave moral and material support to them. The attention paid the city by the Central Committee of the Communist Party of the Soviet Union and by the Soviet government and their concern for her population were constant sources of strength for the Leningraders.

The Central Committee of the Communist Party directed the city's defenders in the struggle from the first day of the siege until the last. Under its leadership the Leningrad party organization headed the defense of the city. It inspired and rallied the defenders to courageous resistance through its energetic labors. The party organization mobilized the population for the construction of the powerful lines of fortifications. In a short time, industry was converted to producing guns, ammunition, and tanks; every available person received military training.

From the onset of the siege, all material resources were distributed to the troops and civilian population through a strictly centralized system, no matter which official agency had title to them. Ration quotas for both the military and civilians were set to accord with the concrete situation as it developed. Top priorities were given to those sectors of military or economic activity that were decisive during any given period.

In the terrible year 1919 when the forces of intervention and the White Guards were trying to strangle the young Soviet republic, Lenin wrote:

> In Petrograd the workers have long since had to shoulder more burdens than the workers in other industrial centers. Both hunger and military danger and the best workers being pulled out for Soviet duty all over Russia: the proletariat of "Piter" has suffered more from all this than the proletariat elsewhere.
>
> And yet we see not the slightest despondency, not the slightest decline in strength among the workers of "Piter." On the contrary. They have been hardened. They have found new strength. They are bringing up fresh fighters. They are accomplishing the mission of a forward detachment excellently, sending help and support wheresoever it is needed most.[1]

[1] V. I. Lenin, *Works*, XXX, 30.

More than two decades had passed since that time. Once more the working class of every country saw the bravery of the workers of "Piter" in the face of terrible danger, saw them splendidly accomplish their mission as a forward detachment and remain, as always, true to Lenin's precepts.

The blockade affected millions of lives. Every Leningrader looked death in the face; there were few among them who did not lose a relative or close friend. But no one grumbled that life had dealt badly with him, and no one complained. All of them rallied around the Communist party and the Soviet government, giving them their trust and going out at their call to deadly battle.

From the vantage point of future years, the heroic deeds of the stalwart defenders of the great city will be seen ever more clearly. Eternal glory to those who fell in battle for the honor and freedom of the motherland!

The war ended. Without letting up, the Leningraders worked tirelessly under difficult conditions to rebuild housing, factories, and municipal transportation. The wounds inflicted by the Fascists on the city were serious and bleeding. Eight hundred and forty industrial plants, forty-four kilometers of water piping, and seventy-five kilometers of the sewer system had been destroyed; Hydroelectric Station Number 8, with an output of 200,000 kilowatts, was completely demolished. But the worst damage was in housing. Over three thousand houses burned or were otherwise destroyed; seven thousand were damaged, and nine thousand wooden houses had been dismantled for firewood. Leningrad lost more than five million square meters of living space. Hundreds of thousands of people were homeless. Yet by the end of 1948 the Leningraders completely restored the ruined buildings and were simultaneously carrying out new residential and municipal construction projects.

By the beginning of 1960, blocks of multistoried stone housing had replaced the wooden houses that had burned or been dismantled. More than two hundred kilometers of water lines were newly built, and the length of the heating-system pipelines exceeded 316 kilometers, in contrast to the seventy kilometers of

1940. The splendid subway from Avtovo to the Finland Station was constructed, with a total length of sixteen kilometers which comfortable trains traverse in a few minutes, carrying more than 350,000 people every day. Around and inside the city new parks and gardens were laid out. Industrial enterprises turned out the most modern machinery and equipment, with a gross product more than three times that of 1940. Many kindergartens, crèches, and schools were built. The population of Leningrad rose above the prewar level to reach 3,400,000.

The entire Soviet people joined Leningrad in a joyous celebration of the city's two hundred and fiftieth anniversary. The city is infinitely dear to every Soviet person. Here the great leader of the proletariat, V. I. Lenin, carried on his revolutionary activity. Here was formed the Soviet government, headed by Lenin, of the first country in the world with a proletarian dictatorship. After the death of Lenin, the Second All-Union Congress of Soviets in 1924 passed a decree changing the city's name from Petrograd to Leningrad. "Henceforth," it said in the decree, "let this greatest center of proletarian revolution be linked forever with the name of the greatest of the leaders of the proletariat, Vladimir Ilyich Ulyanov (Lenin)."

The Leningraders bear this glorious name with just pride. When the enemy raised his sword over the city, Leningrad's men and women, old and young alike, rose to defend it against the Fascist hordes.

Many of them died the death of heroes but they did not let fall the banner of Lenin. They carried it proudly through every ordeal, and the nation will always celebrate their heroic deeds, their selflessness, and courage. Nor are the graves of the fighters who fell during the blockade forgotten. Trees and flowers have been planted at the cemeteries. A memorial monument has been erected at the Piskarevski Cemetery. In the center, on a granite pedestal, rises a six-meter bronze statue of a woman, personifying the motherland. In the middle of the square an eternal flame burns in memory of the dead fighters and toilers. And everyone who crosses the threshold of the sanctuary or passes by the graves bows his head in deep respect and gratitude to those who perished for the honor and independence of their native land.

The heroic achievement of the Leningraders will never fade. It calls and will continue to call new generation after new generation to the task of increasing the glory of our great motherland, her material and spiritual riches, and her fighting and revolutionary traditions.

CHRONOLOGY

1941

September	4	Artillery bombardment of Leningrad begins.
September	8	Capture of Schluesselburg by the Germans. Blockade of Leningrad begins. First mass air attack on the city.
September	12	Reduction in civilian bread, meat, and cereals rations. First vessels arrive at Osinovets with provisions from eastern shore of Lake Ladoga.
September	29	Front stabilized around Leningrad.
October	1	Reduction in civilian bread ration and military rations.
November	8	Soviet troops evacuate Tikhvin. Reduction in military rations.
November	13	Reduction in civilian rations.
November	16	Delivery of provisions to Leningrad by air begins.
November	20	Reduction in civilian bread rations and other rations. Traffic begins to move across lake over ice road.
December	9	Rout of German forces around Tikhvin. Tikhvin liberated from invaders.
December	25	First increase in civilian bread ration under siege conditions.

1942

January	1	Through railroad traffic as far as Voibokalo-Zhikharevo begins.
January	24	Second increase in civilian and military bread rations.
February	10	Branch railroad line from Voibokalo to Kabona goes into operation.
February	11	Increase in civilian food rations.
December	22	By edict of Presidium of Supreme Soviet of USSR "Medal for the Defense of Leningrad" is instituted.

1943

January	18	Blockade broken through. Leningrad and Volkhov fronts link up.
February	6	First train over newly built railroad through corridor of breakthrough arrives in Leningrad.

1944

January	14–27	Leningrad freed completely from enemy blockade.

INDEX